INDIA ENGLISH.

An Autobiography

JILLIAN HASLAM

1

COMMENTS ABOUT INDIAN. ENGLISH

"I had the privilege of working with Jillian Haslam in the late 1990's, when I was the CEO of Bank of America in India. She was President of the Bank of America Charity & Diversity Network and was an outstanding worker in every way, one of the best in my banking career of 35 years. I thought I knew Jillian well — until I read her book, Indian.English. During the years I worked with her, I had absolutely no inkling of what she had gone through in her life, given her professionalism, optimism and stoic dedication to her work. Jillian's book is poignant, sad and at the same time hopeful and uplifting. Her own life has been exemplary in many ways; her capacity to deal with adversity seems immeasurable. I was very much affected by the book, in a positive way. I am certain every reader will find inspiration and lessons from this hard-hitting autobiography and will learn even more when listening to her telling her story of how she goes from a life of nothing to achieving unbelievable success"

– **Ambi Venkateswaran, Consultant, Aozora Bank Ltd., Tokyo (Formerly, Managing Director & North Asia Regional Head, Bank of America Corporation**

"A startling account of an English/Indian family which stayed in India after Indian independence and suffered through excruciating times, losing several children, the girls suffering abuse while living in conditions on the margin of slums and homelessness. Amazing to learn from such real life experiences, it shows how the past does not have to determine ones future"

— **Tom Groenfeldt, Freelance journalist, NYC, USA**

3

"This is the story of an ordinary woman with extraordinary courage. Brought up in the hustle and bustle of Calcutta, Jillian Haslam has recorded her earliest memories in this book – the struggles and abuse she faced while growing up, heartaches of loss and the many obstacles she had to overcome in making life positive for herself and for others. But at the end of it all, she comes across as a person who has unbelievably gained by all the negatives in her life. Not many emerge from such hardship & deprivation with such a positive attitude towards life. What she has learned from her own life and from her studies, she applies to helping others cope with the vicissitudes of fortune. Truly a remarkable person with a remarkable story to tell"

— **Neil O'Brien, Former member of Parliament (India)**

INDIAN.ENGLISH., Jillian Haslam's unforgettable memoir, makes Slumdog Millionaire look like the fantasy it is. Strange as it may seem, there is much hope on display in the book, a living testament to the true heart of the author herself, who survived a hopeless childhood in the slums of Calcutta. Jillian is a saintly spirit who has kept her mind upon the end that endures. She remains one of the only people I have personally ever met whose greatest dream in life is to help others escape oppression and miserable circumstances. Knowing where she came from and how she accomplished it makes me know he will realise her life's work. The words 'cannot recommend her highly enough' are not high enough recommendation for her. A kind, compassionate, honest, loving, and giving lady."

— **Manuel Freedman, Filmmaker, Author. MFM, Los Angeles, CA, USA**

ACKNOWLEDGEMENTS

This book is dedicated with all my love to:
My Father,
Roland Terrance Haslam

My Mother,
Margaret Althea Haslam

All my siblings, who endured and came through some of
the worst times with me, especially to:
Donna
Vanessa
Neil
Susan

My Niece, Jillian, who is named after me, for the love and
happiness she has brought back into all our lives.

My friend and guide through the creation, writing, and
preparation of my book, Manuel.

All Anglo-Indians around the world who I'm sure who can
relate to my story in some small way.

And finally,
To all those who suffer from hardship, poverty and
discrimination for no fault of their own.

Table of Contents

FOREWORD:

During our journey together – for that is what we are undertaking – you might begin thinking about the conditions under which you have always lived and comparing them with mine.

I cannot promise an absence of pain; I do not seek sympathy.

The fact is, that just in the revelation, the telling of the story; it makes me sad about prejudice, sad about people. Most importantly it makes me sad for those poor children throughout the world who, at this very moment you read these words, are made to suffer like my siblings and I did.

It takes a kind of indefatigable energy and ability to care for people at one's own personal sacrifice. I trust you will not be overwhelmed by a dense heaviness after reading my story. Make no mistake: the agony is not the entire tale. Hope percolates through like lava beneath its surface.

We faced a lot during those years and, to be honest, putting it in writing and actually living it are totally different experiences. Compared to your life, perhaps what we had been through virtually all our lives may seem like nothing. If that is the case, I sympathise deeply. We would have a bond, you and I. A bond that knows what the public does not know – that most never have to live through. It was far worse than what you, I, or anyone could have written about.

We dwelt in circumstances beyond harsh poverty and abject hardship. We suffered severe racism and abuse – words that are not used or known where I grew up. Many of those who inflicted this pain would never even have thought of it as abuse, merely that it was what people do there, out of ignorance or weakness. Nevertheless, the humiliation and hurt we suffered was a million times worse than anything I have ever encountered since.

I am a product of two cultures. One could say I was born in the wrong place at the wrong time. One can make excuses for just about anything. Let it suffice to say that, being an Anglo-Indian in India, born long after India's 1947 independence from Britain, remains a unique and harrowing experience.

I was born in the city of Calcutta. I left India in 2000 and now reside in the United Kingdom.

My book examines many emotions and events that may seem lost or unimportant, but within these pages, it is my desire that you feel the upside, the positive, the uplifting;

8

what American President Abraham Lincoln called 'the better angels' of our nature.

For every atrocity described here, there is, perhaps, a parallel kindness. One cannot overlook the small, the seemingly insignificant, the daily, the mundane. Within what most people would label small and ordinary things, normal events, and regular people, thrives a grace beyond description that literally saves lives every day.

Kindness sometimes triumphs in the face of impossible odds. In the grim and grimy slums of Calcutta where we huddled underneath a stairway, people helped us. Among the hardened, violent, and ugly streets that define the worst parts of post-colonial India, brutality and human kindness waltzed in a slow and intricate dance. I can hear the mystery of that particular music when I revisit the land of my birth, especially among the lowest of the low—the 'Indian-English.'

I want nothing more than to help people change their lives, especially those who have been through dire circumstances and events that most often can destroy them. I have set out to prove to you that your circumstances do not need to become your reality. In the words of Maya Angelou: 'I can be changed by what happens to me, but I refuse to be reduced by it.'

I have changed my life, and want to help as many as I can to do the same. That is all I want. Hence my telling of this story.

If I can make a difference to as many people as I can, through my work, I would die a happy person. I do not really need more.

CHAPTER ONE:
INDIAN. ENGLISH.

In a world that has many victims, I am a victim. My story may read like a chronicle of some of the world's worst abuses, like discrimination, social injustice, and living in conditions that human beings can barely endure. Despite the presence of much sorrow, revealing this all to you makes me feel a deep love and abiding hope, yet will force many to ask: why do people treat others so inhumanely?

The answer is that everything is done through weakness or ignorance, and never intentionally. I insist that people are not their behaviours; a difficult concept, but it is absolutely true.

When I was growing up in India, Anglo-Indians were a small community. Many had already emigrated. We looked different, both physically and in our style of dress, as well as in our outlook on life.

Outcasts, non-castes, castaways – whatever you like. We were like ghosts. We were either visible but non-existent, or existent but invisible. Our heritage, colouring, religion and very being put a target on our foreheads, giving total license for the Indian men in our slums to do with us whatever they wished to do. You will see below how this impacted my sisters and me. Stamped in blood upon the bull's eye of that target were the words: Indian. English.

My siblings and I were vanishing remnants of a bygone era. Our social consciousness and identities were mostly ignored, if not wholly suppressed. There was no place in the hierarchy of Indian society for us – even at the bottom. Essentially, we were non-existent, and many wished for that to be absolutely true, especially we ourselves.

We struggled constantly with problems involved in emotional and cultural integration. We were not even given a representation similar to the Scheduled Tribe Quota. This highlighted how much of a minority we really were. Or was it really just the fact that we were not wanted there and therefore did not exist in the eyes of anyone, including the government?

Anglo-Indian is a much maligned and much abused term, to the extent that even the Oxford English dictionary has four possible meanings for the term. It began in reference to the children of British soldiers or traders who had the fortune (!) of growing up in India as a result of their parents moving there. There are, of course, many famous examples, prominent among whom would be

Rudyard Kipling and Jim Corbett. By the time the British left India in 1947, a majority of Anglo-Indians had gone west in search of greener (and as I discover now, wetter!) pastures.

By 1947, the term had been appropriated by the erstwhile Eurasians who were the poorer cousins, normally with a British father and a local mother. Of course, latterly, anyone with a slightly Christian-sounding name in India, or, even the odd foreign-born person who thought it would be good to be associated with Britain, proudly refers to oneself as an Anglo-Indian. This action of somewhat dubious ethics is sometimes responsible for the poor view of our community held in general Indian society. My father always claimed that some of them, who, once they had decided to agree to be proselytized by the missionaries, began appropriating names from headstones in the nearest graveyard and started to call themselves Anglo-Indians.

Most history books fail to recount some things, however, in all the melee of Indian independence and the mass exodus of the majority of the British and Anglo-Indians. History books are by their nature selective, and Eurasians were a minority of no importance.

There were an unfortunate few genuine Anglo-Indian

families, who either chose to remain in India, or were forced to do so due to health reasons or by financial constraints. These are the ones who ended up growing up there, lost in the streets of Calcutta amongst the teeming millions. My parents were one such unfortunate couple, and this is my story of growing up in that environment.

In order for me to reach out to realise my goal, these pages probe the composition of what some people call the journey of the soul. They will explore:

· A family's humble struggles;
· The human propensity for cruelty;
· Hatred stirred by ignorance;
· The shrapnel of love;
· Squalor;
· Magnificence;
· Heartaches of loss;
· Obligation;
· Headaches of daily life;
· The juxtaposition of values inherent in class warfare;
· Discrimination;
· Determination;
· Abuses too many to name—some for which there even are no names;
· The capacity to overcome and to heal.

14

My sincere hope remains that the challenges of my life so far – my 'cross to bear', to use my late father's words – inspires those who need inspiration, soothes those ruptured by intolerance, and identifies ongoing, racial and social discrimination and violence that plague the face of the earth today, now; every single hour of every single day.

I am humbled to be tasked to do written justice to the story of my life. I have no idea how I will accomplish it; but it will be an honour to give whatever I've got in my soul to make it my best effort.

More than anything, I hope these pages serve.

CHAPTER TWO:

THE INTERSECTION OF TWO HEARTS

My father, Roland Terrance Haslam, was born on the 16th of January 1922, in Calcutta, to British parents, who themselves were each a child of British parents on both sides. He grew up during the Raj in Calcutta and joined the British Army at a very young age – I think, if I recall correctly, that he was seventeen or eighteen when he joined. At the time his parents' family did well, because his own father had been in the British Services too.

My dad joined the army and married his first wife, whom I believe was a very gentle and loving woman. They had many children together. His first wife was also born to British parents. My father explained that their marriage began to fall into problems when the kids were quite grown-up, but she had rarely, if ever, allowed him to discipline them. My father, being from the army, saw discipline and exemplary behaviour as the only way to a good life, and could not understand or accept this passion of hers. He must have resented the helplessness he felt from not being able to caution or control his own children. For the sake of protecting the children from becoming a battleground, they separated.

On our side, however, it was completely different. My mother felt that discipline was everything, and compulsory in the upbringing of children. Of course, this disposition of hers suited my father very well. She allowed him to discipline us and to make decisions in our lives. She gave him the required freedom to do what he was good at doing.

My mother was one of four children, whose father was Scottish and mother Armenian. Her first husband had abandoned her with two small children. She had been forced to marry him when she was just seventeen years old, because my grandmother thought he was a good man. They had also just lost my grandfather, and my grandmother – who was terminally ill herself at the time – was worried about leaving my mother defenceless, vulnerable and alone.

Being very young, single and, above all, foreign in India, would have no doubt left my mother open to dangers that she was not prepared for. My mother always said that her brother would be of no help or protection to her, since he was self-absorbed and did not pay attention to family. Making maximum use of his good looks, he lived a playboy lifestyle to which he became addicted.

17

According to my mother, my grandmother thought she had protected her by forcing her to marry so young. She considered her first husband to be a good man, and never worried about his upbringing or integrity. He spoke English and came across very well, and that is what mattered to my grandmother. But this was not to be my mother's future security.

To begin with, her first husband was not British, and by no means Anglo-Indian, and had no British blood whatsoever. I guess things like this are where my father's rant about people adopting Christian names and Anglo identities from the closest headstone came from. He tricked my mother into believing he was heading to Britain on an assignment. Papers in hand, Anderson left for the UK by ship, leaving her in utter poverty, with a promise that he would send for her as soon as he settled down in the UK. She did not hear from him ever again.

My mother then met my father. There was a twenty-two year age gap between them. Altogether they had nine children, but four died within the first year of their births. Of the ones who survived, I'm the second eldest.

The values, the qualities, the virtues each and everyone of us possesses today, has everything to do with both my parents. This was due, to a large degree, because my mother hardly ever got in the way of discipline. She was steady as a rock in supporting my father's directions for our lives. They both gave all of us constant love and affection to balance the discipline, creating an environment which made us well-grounded and secure.

When he served in the British Army, my father had travelled to countries like Oman, Iraq, Iran, and many others. I remember him showing me a certificate of exemplary service in the army, which I have with me even today. He had faced a lot in India. While he always felt that he was there on a mission but certainly would one day settle in England, fate proved otherwise.

Due to health reasons, he had to remain in India. My mother had two older brothers who I believe left India and moved to the UK soon after independence. Sadly, in time she lost touch with both of them; another disappointment which never really left her. She passed away wanting nothing more than to be reunited with them but, unfortunately, this was not to be. The same was the case with my father, who wanted nothing more than to see his sister one last time. Sadly, however, just as I was planning a visit for him to the UK to see his sister, he passed away.

Against their true hearts' desires, my parents remained in India for the rest of their lives.

Jill's father

Jill's mother

CHAPTER THREE:
SISTERS AND BROTHERS

My parents went on to have nine children, four of whom were not destined to live past a month or two. We lost twins Kimberley and Alan and two other girls, Mini and Carol. Four girls and one boy survived.

My father, after having left the army, joined a Company called MRF Tyres where he was a mechanical engineer. They were one of the biggest companies that made tyres in India. For a number of years during this period, our household became stabilised for the first time.

My elder siblings, along with Geoffrey and Barbara, who were from my mother's first husband, were away at boarding school for most of the time. Both Geoffrey and Barbara were doing very well, although they had had a tough childhood because of my mother's first husband. My father provided for them as often as he could. He gave them a home to come to whenever they returned from boarding school, and did what he could with the resources he had at the time.

I was born at home one morning, around nine o'clock, in a room located on a street called Totties Lane, in the city of Calcutta. As the story goes, my elder siblings were in school and my father was dressed, ready to go to work, when my mother was forced to give birth to me at home. A nurse who lived close by, Ms Jenny Kirk, helped with my birth. She was later, in sheer gratitude, made my godmother. Though I have never met her, I love and thank her for helping my mother in her time of need. It was just before me, I believe, that Carol was born, but did not survive past a couple of months due to a series of illnesses and malnutrition.

My sister Mini was born after me but did not survive past a few months either, for the same reasons as Carol. Vanessa, my younger sister, was born two years after me. She survived, despite the difficult conditions she was born into as a result of the financial constraints my parents were operating under. The instability with which my parents constantly grappled began to grow in leaps and bounds, as my father now had many more to feed and only one job to support the household. This, coupled with the death of their two infants and Vanessa's birth, caused a great deal of worry to both of my parents. They were forced to move to a new home multiple times, and were never able to settle down as families should. At around 50 years of age, my father was a relatively young and healthy, man when the stresses of his life mounted up and caused him his first heart attack. I was about four years old then, and didn't quite understand what had happened.

Calcutta today is not what it used to be. New suburban districts have sprung up, expanding the city in all directions. Most of central Calcutta, however, remains the same. Names like Free School Street, Park Street and Ripon Street still ring a bell for me. Although very many names were changed once the British left, just like the name of the main metropolitan cities have now been changed.

The neighbourhood we grew up in was varied and cosmopolitan. It consisted of Indian families, mixed families, and families like ours. Facilities and cleanliness in the neighbourhood was hard to come by. Parks and playgrounds were not even thought of. As a result, several families, including my own, decided to send their children to boarding school at very young ages to be given a good English education and to mix with like-minded children. It was also with an attempt to take them off the streets and keep them away from other dangers.

Due to financial constraints, we were sometimes left in boarding school for months on end. We were sometimes lucky if we came home even once a year. When we did go

23

home it was only for very short periods, and I remember my parents being very strict. We were not allowed to spend much time outside our house or mix with the locals. My parents felt that the streets of Calcutta were no place for young children to be, especially young girls. There were too many men who would be happy to prey on little girls who looked different, and who were vulnerable in such a locality.

Not much has changed in the Calcutta I knew by way of cleanliness or safety. The streets are still the same, if not worse now. The footpaths are covered with litter and blotted in spit, chewed tobacco, chewed up betel-leaf juice or cigarette butts. The stench of urine is everywhere. The roads are used by many as toilets. However, in contrast to the environment, the warmth and affection of the people in Calcutta makes one want to keep returning there.

Boarding schools were a safe haven for Anglo-Indian families such as ours. They were clean, safe, and, most importantly, free for the children of ex-British servicemen. These schools were set up by the British in Victorian times and were modelled to mirror the education system back in Britain. After the British left India, funds were raised from people who lived abroad, and ongoing sponsorships of boarding, lodging and education were arranged for all such children. This enabled kids like us to obtain a high standard of English education in a clean and safe environment. I shall always be grateful to those who sponsored my siblings and I, for without them we would not be where we are today.

Before any of my siblings and I were big enough to be admitted to boarding school, we moved home virtually every eight to ten months. Most often my mother requested people to keep us, or we stayed in little rooms which were situated in squalor, where the rent was little or nothing. We managed to live separated for days on end from each other because the people who agreed to keep us didn't have big enough houses to keep all of us. Some kept Vanessa & myself, some kept my elder sister, and some kept Mum – and that is how we managed, for years on end. We never really had much to move, and at most often had only two or three bags to carry.

I remember how my mother once took us straight to one of my father's friends, Noel and Eleanor Samuels. My memory of them is that they were very kind to us, and I can still remember Mrs Samuels feeding her children and Vanessa and I from a single plate. This family shared everything they had. I have never forgotten how kind and loving they were to us, even though we had absolutely nothing to give them in return. They kept my mum with us too so that we were not parted from each other, and also kept my dad once he got better and came out of hospital. We must have stayed with them for several months, but it wasn't possible for Mr Samuels and his wife to keep us for any length of time, since they themselves didn't have very much. Despite that, they never, ever, in the slightest instance hinted at us overstaying our welcome, which left my parents tasked to find a place for us to stay once again.

My mother went to see the kindly gentleman, Mr Nazareth, who offered them their positions in a place called Dum Dum. He always had a bag full of 'Muri Balls' which were balls made out of bloated rice and jaggery (unrefined sugar). They were sweet and light, and my younger sister and I relished them when we went to see him.

There we were; two children growing up in a neighbourhood that was dangerous and rife with squalor. My father had his heart attack, and things went from somewhat okay to difficult. That is when my parents got an opportunity to leave Calcutta and move to Dum Dum, a rural town just outside Calcutta.

This happened through their acquaintance with a man called Mr. Nazareth, who had a wealthy friend. He wanted to use some money borrowed from this friend to fund and set up a small school for Indian children to learn English. He employed my parents to set up and run the school for him. Dad would be the principal of the school, and Mum a teacher. My parents were offered a fair salary, quarters, and a free education for their children. They had also moved our household several times due to financial constraints, had lost two children, and had another two very young children to consider. They were also concerned about my sister Donna, who was very young and very attractive and, as a result, was unsafe in their current environment. With dwindling funds and too many mouths to feed, my parents saw this opportunity as a godsend, and accepted the appointment immediately.

My older siblings, except for Donna, were in boarding school at the time, and so my mother, father, Donna, Vanessa and I moved to Dum Dum to begin our new life. My parents worked hard at setting up the school and were successful in building it on the same model as the schools the British had set up in India. It helped to restore a sense of stability at a very crucial and much-appreciated time.

People ask how I feel writing and talking about all of this today. Does it make me angry? It did. However, to relive it and to deal with it as an adult, rather than as a frightened little child, is different; while, at the same time, unbelievable still.

As I trained to become a Life Coach and Motivational Trainer, I learnt a lot about the human mind and how it influences one's actions. I was able to understand a lot more about myself and relate to my experiences better. It is this learning and understanding from my own experiences that has helped me reach out and help many others with their challenges and problems. It convinced me that life could be improved with the right learning and guidance. I have abandoned being afraid of these ingrained traumas. Instead, I have worked towards understanding them, to deal with and dispel them as fears that do not have control over my life today. As in the words of Mark Caine: 'The first step towards success is taken when you refuse to be a captive of the environment in which you first find yourself.'

Jill and her Siblings

Neil & Susan

Donna

Vanessa & Jillian

CHAPTER FOUR:
DUM DUM

INDIAN. ENGLISH. Exotic as it may sound to some ears, I cannot say it is a mark of positive distinction. I always think that, if we were not in that country – if we were born in the West, if we were born somewhere else – many of us would have been able to establish broader foundations for success in life. But we never got that kind of opportunity. In the long run, we must all be stronger for it, in the way that adversity builds character.

The distinctive traits, certainly not of all I.E. but of many, is our fair skin-colour, followed by the accent with which we speak English. The outgrowth for this choice is that the inflection of our accents created a distinguishing linguistic element. In many respects, it perversely served to alienate us more than if we had spoken perfect Hindi, Bengali or any other Indian language. Were you to speak to us on the telephone, you would not be able to tell that we Haslams were, for the most part, fair-skinned English people.

Within seven or eight months, the school in Dum Dum was running and everything had settled down. My father had recovered from the heart attack. Though my parents were not paid a lot, they were grateful for the stability. The twins, Kimberly and Alan, were born and we were enjoying a much-deserved sense of comfort and harmony.

My earliest and most pleasant childhood memories are from when my family and I were in Dum Dum. I recall how proud my parents were of what they had accomplished after a lot of hardship and pain, even though it was nothing much at all. Their intention was to make a difference, and they were. Here lay the haven where they could build and mould something of their own, away from the stresses and dangers of the city. Fate, however, had planned something else for us entirely.

Very soon into the assignment, we were to be robbed of our happiness. Naxalites got wind of us and an attack was imminent. One of us in particular was the unwitting and unfortunate catalyst of a protracted series of dire events that haunts all of us to this day. These events were triggered by the colour of our skin and a misunderstood foreign outlook within a small-minded, closed, native community.

The sacrificial lamb was my beautiful sister, Donna. In 1968, a Maoist faction waged a rebellion in the West Bengal district of Naxalbari. Known as 'Naxalites', they began to infiltrate politics in Calcutta and to influence it in many ways. They won seats on the government. Being the independent Communist party of India, they took their politics to the people of the outlying villages. The Naxalites slowly seized control of most villages and by the mid-1970s pervasively wielded that power with often-deadly force. Feared by all, they were criminals who ran an area and its people. They were a community of terrorists in the rural outskirts of West Bengal.

Dum Dum, being extremely remote, was alien to white people. The arrival of our family and, in particular, of my teenage sister Donna, didn't go unnoticed. She was blonde, very fair and had blue eyes. Word about us and mainly about her had spread through the villages. My father was six foot two, extremely fair, and the local people looked upon him as a god of some sort.

Unfortunately, it didn't stop there. Word got as far as the Naxalites, and when they saw Donna, they wanted her for their own. Her days were numbered. She was to be kidnapped.

My parents had built up a good relationship with the people in the area, despite not being able to speak the local language fluently, and were tipped off about Donna's threatened abduction. A local man, who did not want his name to be mentioned, had heard that this was going to be the case from another person, and relayed what he had heard. They were terrified and knew that the Naxalites would stop at nothing to achieve what they set out to achieve.

The plot to abduct Donna had already been hatched by the time my parents were informed. They were warned not to speak a word about it; to act as though everything was normal, and not to attract any attention to themselves. By doing so, they ran the risk of the whole family being murdered. For years after it had happened, I remember my mother telling us the story and not being able to control her tears.

She never forgot the dread—that all it might have taken was for someone to want to look good in the eyes of one called Banu Bose, the Leader of the Naxalites, and to have informed them of our move. She was terrified and my father could not believe just how difficult and dangerous our lives had become.

My parents were given a plan to get out of the village under cover of darkness. I remember my mother telling me that they stayed up all night, praying that all of us would not suddenly be killed, hoping that it wasn't a plot of some kind but a genuinely kind gesture on the part of some local villager whom they would never meet again. To send just my sister away would mean death for either all of us, or certainly for both my parents. Another possibility loomed - the kidnap of both us little girls (myself and my sister Vanessa) as revenge, since kidnappers, murderers and robbers infiltrated the area. Agonisingly, my parents had to be very, very careful.The police of the area would not interfere. They were too scared of these Naxalites and would not act against them to protect anyone.

The plan was to take nothing with us. Everything we owned was to be left behind. All the hard work put in, and all the effort made, had to be left behind. My parents were crushed; their lives and family uprooted again. Their feeling of devastation is not possible to adequately describe. For what remained behind with their belongings were two priceless possessions.

They had not quite recovered from the deaths of Mini and Carol who had passed away in Calcutta just before they left for Dum Dum – and they were now trying to deal with the deaths of the twins they had lost in Dum Dum itself, Kimberley and Alan, who had died but a few weeks before. Not only that trauma, but also the trauma of having to bury their own children in large tea-leaf boxes because they couldn't afford coffins.

Donna was old enough to understand about the twins passing, whom she had grown to love dearly. She could not bear the thought of leaving them in Dum Dum. It seemed a sacrilegious act of defilement to their memories to abandon them to the Naxalites and to never be able to go and visit even their graves again.

We didn't have the time to even say goodbye to the twins. That thought, even today, haunts me. I am sure that, although my parents never talked about it, it hurt more than words could ever explain. The greatest loss any human being can suffer is the loss of one's own child. Not to mention losing four due to malnutrition as a result of extreme poverty.

I remember the twins were so tiny, and when Kimberley died first my elder sister Donna cried, holding her like she was going to die herself. I have never, in all my work with children throughout my life, ever seen the type of grief and sadness I saw on my sister's face on the nights on which they died.

My mother knew that Kimberley had died. Despite spending hours together, however, she could not tell Donna that this was the case. She waited for Dad to get home so that she would have him there before breaking the news to Donna. She just kept telling her, "Don't try and pick her up, let her sleep." She also knew that one would not survive without the other, whuch was true enough. Alan died a few days later.

The house was just unbearably sad. I remember my mother trying to tell us stories in order for us not to worry, but the despair and the grief that each of us felt cannot be explained. Even though she tried hard to keep a brave face herself, she sometimes broke down and walked outside, pretending she needed to think about something. We knew, of course, that the sadness on her face said it all. I remember asking my mother why she was crying, to which she answered that she wasn't crying but only had a bad cold, so her eyes were watering.

A local man had brought us a tea-leaf case, which was made out of wood and sealed with tape at the ends. I remember Mum turning it around so that the open part faced her like a little doll's house with the doors open. In that she put an old sheet, and then Donna placed her own little pillow into it because she wanted Kimberley to have it forever. I can still picture her pink lips; she had such an angelic face. I remember Mum trying to seal the box and Donna getting hysterical, saying "You'll suffocate her!" and Dad holding her while Mum kept taping the box. I do not know how she did it or how she managed to seal her little daughter in, but she did. I'll never know how Dad was able to pick up the box, but he did, and he walked through the doors.

There was no funeral. My mother couldn't go to the burial, because women weren't allowed in the area where they had found a little pit in which to lay her to rest. My mum kept saying to my dad, "Take me one day, and just show me where you put her." Unfortunately, that was never to be. People were most often cremated, and therefore we didn't know of any cemeteries in Dum Dum. More likely, I think my father did not want my mother to know that that was indeed the case.

Young as I was, I could tell that things were not like a normal burial should have been. Still, Dad said, "It was nice...she's okay." But he never provided any description at all. In fact, he was so disturbed that he hardly spoke for weeks after. Until this day, I think he died knowing how terrible it really was to not only go through something like that, but to accept the conditions that went with it. He never did speak a word about it to my mother, in fear that it would hurt her terribly. Throughout my life, I cannot help but think of how hard it must have been for him to keep silent about something like that; and, what's more, how honourable a human being he was to suffer it alone.

They had to go through it yet again when Alan died a few days later. All I can remember is running to the door to see Dad walking with this box in his hands, two locals following him, since there wasn't even a car or any type of conveyance at the time.

I may have been little, yet I could tell that my mother was existing solely because of us, and not because she wanted to. Even today when I try to talk about it, I am unable to explain what we actually felt. Vanessa and I were only children, holding two other dead children and watching them as they were being laid out in large tea-leaf cases, being taken away, never to be seen again.

The pain and the depression felt by my elder sister Donna was what I believed turned her into the emotional person that she is. The mere thought of losing someone even to this day is unbearable for her. I have been with people who have had losses, but with her it is a trauma that has never been resolved. She would not eat for days, she refused to have their things touched, and sobbed virtually every hour of every day. She has refused to have children of her own, and never talks about it.

I now understand how such traumatic childhood incidents can continue to impact on?? a person even many years later, and I am trying in my own way to use my training as a life coach to help her move on. Yet, like with my father, we cannot fathom nor understand the true depth of that experience or the lasting impact it had on all our lives, though mainly on hers.

Vanessa and I just stood by and cried, primarily because we relied on Donna as our big sister. To see her break down was not easy on us. But never to see the baby twins again was something we were too little to comprehend. We heard the word 'death', but we couldn't fully understand what it meant. All we did know is that they were never coming home again, and Mum said that she was sending them to Jesus.

I am sure that, for any parent, the loss of a child is the hardest thing to face. How overwhelming can it be, then, to lose four children due to extreme poverty and being incapable to save them, especially after having cared for them for some time? It is something beyond all expression. All this in addition to fighting for survival – and now fleeing for our lives, in a country which was against us, all the while living in utter poverty.

Without ceremony or our ability to adequately prepare or say good-bye to the twins, the time had come to escape from Dum Dum.

CHAPTER FIVE:

THE TRAIN OF NO RETURN

I can clearly remember that night. It must have been about one in the morning, maybe two. I remember we were awakened from sleep and we were told to quickly and to silently put on our shoes. They dressed Donna in an Indian outfit to disguise her. My mother dressed in dark clothing that fully covered her. She told us to take some bottles of water in our pockets.

Two local people from the area led us out through the fields and along the woods in the darkness. Customarily, in that part of the world, interfering or helping an intended victim meant the death to oneself and one's family if found out. I will always be grateful to those kind souls who risked their own lives to save ours.

I remember it was very, very dark, and Vanessa and I were holding hands really tightly. We were led out in a queue. First the people who were helping us, then Donna, then Vanessa and me, and then my parents. I remember that Vanessa and I – six and fouryears of age – walked as quietly and quickly as our little feet would take us.

I remember my mother saying, "Hold hands and do not

let go no matter what happens. Jillian look after Vanessa. If I say run, I mean run, and do not look back for me. Do not stop. I need you to know that whatever happens, both your father and me love you very much and always will. So I need you to promise me that you'll run when I say so. Do not worry where you go. Just keep running!"

Her words terrified me – partly because I couldn't understand why she wouldn't tell us where to run to, and partly because of the fear and tension I saw on my parents' faces. All I did know was that there was something very serious about to happen. Being partly asleep, partly awake and partly taking instructions, I can still feel Vanessa's little hand trembling in mine.

We started to walk very slowly through some kind of fields which were pitch dark. I felt myself stopping sometimes and my mother gently pushing my head, as if to say "keep going." This walk might have gone on for a good twenty to thirty minutes, with Vanessa and myself continuously stopping to see if we were alone or if my mother was still there. I think our little hearts could have stopped at any moment, we were so afraid.

After we got through the fields, we got into two bicycle rickshaws that were waiting for us. We were then rushed to the station, and when we arrived we boarded the first train out of there.

We had barely escaped with our lives and nothing else, very much like the von Trapp family in The Sound of Music, except in India. However, unlike them, we were totally poverty-stricken. Our very existence was in danger, and the country was harsh and unforgiving. We were out of Dum Dum, but we were still at risk.

The train reached its destination halfway to Calcutta, and we had to get off this train and wait to board the next one to Calcutta. This was much better than waiting in Dum Dum for a train to Calcutta. We had to get out of that area and we did, just barely.

Though we were out of the area, my parents were in no way at rest. Mum and Dad were aware of the long arms of the Naxalites, and were still afraid of them catching up with us.

I remember my mother taking us to a waiting room and making us sit in a dark corner so that we would not attract any attention; even the slightest recognition could be fatally dangerous.

We stayed in the corner until early the next morning, when we boarded the train to Calcutta. In the brightness of day, Donna's fair skin instantly stood out, and the local men were trying their best to get close enough to her to touch her inappropriately. Vanessa and I were holding my mother's skirt as we were told to do, our little heads buried into it.

The train was packed like a tin of sardines. We were scared, tired, hungry and literally suffocating. Donna, too was trying to protect us: because Vanessa and I were so tiny, we were hardly visible, a bit like two small shoots in a forest of Eucalyptus trees. To make matters worse, the temperature was soaring to near forty degrees centigrade. Along with the huge crowd of people, also being transported in the same carriage were big bundles of straw, bundles of wrapped-up clothes, shoes, vegetables, food, tea, chickens in baskets, utensils, rolls of cloth, tins of oil...anything that could be carried.

I remember looking up at Donna as she tried to make some space for us to breathe. She had tears rolling down her cheeks as she tried to fend off the men whilst looking after us. My mother, too, was trying to shield her, while simultaneously trying to look after us.

This is when it all happened...I heard my father saying, "Babe, I can't see a thing." And my mother saying, "Speak up I cannot hear you." And he replied, "Babe, where are you? I cannot see anything at all. It's a complete black-out."

I remember Mum reaching up his six foot two frame in order to grab his short-sleeved white shirt, while trying to hold onto all of us girls at the same time. She was only five foot tall, but she had a will of iron and nerves of steel.

My mother asked, "You can't see anything?" And he said, "I can't see a thing." He had totally lost his eyesight. On such a crowded train, with such a lot of people, it was terrible.

Indomitable, surviving in a blizzard of misery, Mum now kept her hand on his shoulder. She leaned down and told us, intently, "Whatever happens, do not leave my skirt."

Within a few minutes the train arrived at Howrah station in Calcutta, and we attempted to get off the train with hundreds of people, ninety-nine percent of them men, pushing from every angle. They had no care for the women travelling with them, no care for my father, who was clearly in deep distress, and no care for the two tiny little children who were almost getting trampled upon and crushed to death. All they were interested in was trying to touch Donna one last time before they got off the train with their bundles, baskets and chickens. My mother kept her hand on my father's back, and managed to guide him off the train with Donna and the two of us. I remember her pouring with perspiration, but shouting to us again, "Whatever happens, do not leave my skirt!"

We were wrenched toward the exit, each of us trying to look out for the other. With tears streaming down our little faces out of sheer fear of getting lost, we were dreadfully worried about what had happened to my father.

Even at the station we were being trampled on. Men were even trying to touch Vanessa and me. Most of them were chewing pan (an Indian tobacco mixed with leaves that turns the mouth red in colour). That awful smell will never leave me. Donna too was struggling to stay close, trying to watch us and stop the men from touching her and us, all at the same time. Sobbing and trying to protect Vanessa in my own little way, I remember looking up at Donna for help. I saw her face blood-red with temper and tears and hurt. I could tell Donna was feeling totally abused, and was desperately wanting to just hit out somehow.

When the train stopped at Howrah Bridge station, we could not even move. Vanessa and I were totally crushed and couldn't take any more. I only remember that we had just been carried off the train somehow and whisked across the track to the platform in a sea of teeming humanity.

My mother had had to push my father off the train in such a way that he would not land on the gravel between the train and the platform. She did it so that the crowd carried him off the train, and so that she could get us off as well, since Vanessa was too small to get off the train herself.

Then, he vanished. She could not see him, and was trying hard to search through the sea of rushing commuters. She needed to find him. He needed her help.

This was not the end of our journey.

As we rushed along the edge of the platform, my mother was almost running, dragging Vanessa and me as we trying our best to keep up. My mother frantically searched for my father while Donna wept as she tried to get through to watch us, so that neither of us got left behind. It was in all of this furious commotion that I distinctly remember Mum screaming, "Ronnie! Stop!"

We saw my father, who had stopped dead in his tracks. He was almost about to walk straight off the other side of the platform, and would have fallen onto the live track. Her scream caught him in time, preventing him from stepping over the edge. My mother rushed to him and pulled the back of his shirt, guiding him away from the platform edge.

All in all, it was horrific. One of the worst experiences I have ever had, and one that the three of us live with everyday. I cannot re-live this experience without feeling sheer pain for my mother, my father, Donna and for us, all in different ways. I am still apprehensive – and I always have been ever since – of surging, milling crowds.

I remember Vanessa, who was so tiny and so pale, turning as red as a tomato as she emerged from that train, a look of fear, confusion and trauma on her face. With her little toes squeezed inside her sandals, her little feet must have been stood on and crushed at least a thousand times. Like me, she was too little to understand anything and was just doing whatever I did. All she remembers is the horror of the whole nightmarish experience; and, especially, the moment we found my father, with all of us crying but without knowing why. My mother held onto my father, and would not leave him. Donna held my mother, sobbing, while Vanessa was holding onto one of my father's legs with one hand and trying to pull me close with the other, as though she was terrified of losing me. We were traumatised, trembling, crying – and yet grateful, all at the same time.

Beside my father not being able to see, we arrived in Calcutta with no money, no food and nowhere to stay. My mother took my father to The Salvation Army. We came to learn that my father had had a minor heart attack on the train, which was the reason for his blackout and temporary loss of sight. The Salvation Army took care of ex-servicemen, and offered to take care of him. He was very ill. My mother put him there until we could find a place of our own. They would look after him and give him the medication and everything else he needed, completely free of cost. Even today when I pass their place on visits to my sisters in Croydon, it brings back so many memories...many of which are not always easy to confront.

As to my sister, Donna, my mother put her with some friends, because there was no way that she would be safe in the area where my mother was planning to take us. She would be vulnerable in such a place, as men would be drawn to her like bees to honey.

Once my mother knew that Donna was safe, she took us to a local food shop where she fed us by buying one naan bread and a little curry, which Vanessa and myself shared. She had just a cup of tea and said she didn't feel like eating, telling us to finish it because we had a very, very long distance to go (she meant to walk) to see Aunt Barber, who was going to keep us.

CHAPTER SIX:
LIVING UNDER THE STAIRS

My mother then approached two ladies, who she thought were her friends, to keep us, although they really didn't have any proper place to give us. Their building was located in a narrow lane with all kinds of food shops where they sold naan breads, wraps, curries, tea, utensils, and they used the side of the buildings as toilets at the same time. Nothing expensive at all, nothing fancy. It was a place mainly for the lowest class people – the poorest of the poor – to go there and maybe have a whole meal for one or two rupees, depending on what they ate.

It was an extremely bad area, very poor and riddled with crime. In between some of the shops, there were a few totally dilapidated and run-down buildings. The two ladies were in one of these buildings on the upper level, which was reached by a staircase positioned to the left.

Upstairs there were about four or five little rooms, no bigger than six feet square, where other families and these two ladies lived. None too graciously or altruistically, but nonetheless granted to us, they gave my mother a place for us to stay under the steps on the left side (as shown on the cover of the book). We must have been there for about eight months or so, my father seemed to recall later, because that's how long he was kept at the Salvation Army.

Under the steps was just terrible. With a space no bigger than a narrow four-seat dining table, our new home was dark, full of water from holes in the ground, covered in slime and mildew and crawling with vermin. The ground cover beneath the stairs was composed of disintegrating flooring, which had for years and years been in drastic need of repair that had never ever been done. We put plastic down on which to sleep, and used some old kind of bedding that they gave us. Such as it was, the accommodation came to us as a favour, because we were children and had nowhere else to go. But it was a roof above our heads and a shelter from the heat, rain and other dangers. And so that is where we were to stay until my father could recover, get a job, and come to get us out of there.

During this time the two ladies upstairs ruled over us, shouting repeatedly at us. They made us do their bidding – having us do their beds, clean their floors, sending us out with cans to buy tea from a nearby tea shop or to a local grocery store whenever they needed something, even if it meant us running to the shops twenty times a day for something or other they thought they needed.

We lived in public, exposed to anyone passing by on the way to the food shops and to fetch water from a pump, which stood barely a few feet away from our bedding, and served as the supply for hundreds of families. People washed their clothes, spat, and bathed around that pump. It allowed us to get to know many, many people there and from nearby. On many occasions, my mother wouldn't be able to get home to give us anything; the guard from the local cinema hall would bring us some sweets, or made his children share their lunch with us. In due course we seemed to always end up being with them at lunchtime, just so they would share their food with us.

Living like that exposed us to another sickness. Inevitably, we were subjected to the local men, who never failed to try and touch us, abuse us, make lewd signs to us, and call us lurid names. Even as little as we were, every passing man tried in some way or the other to make us sit on their laps and fondle us. I remember a man touching my breasts and then giving me a sweet. I wondered why, but now I understand.

My mother, on the other hand, had it worse than her children. She worked for the ladies in return for the place under the steps, and she was beaten many occasions by both of these ladies for not having done one thing or another. They made up the rules as they went along. Impossible to please by their own devious design, these supposed errors on my mother's part were pure figments of their imaginations. They always looked for something to be wrong, and, finding none, invented something to prompt a beating.

Quite frequently nowadays, I recall how my mother made Vanessa and me little coats that were assembled from cloth fragments and trimmings that she collected from local tailors. They would throw away the pieces from the cloth they cut for shirts, trousers and other articles. She brought it all home (under the stairs) and stitched it together to make clothes and blankets for us.

A constant lack of money forced my mother to go out looking for it whenever she could, and to try to find small jobs around in order to make some. The deal was that she had to spend time with the ladies helping and working for them. She would cook, scrub, clean, wash and run errands. They wouldn't pay her, because it was in return for giving us the place under the steps. Pressure mounted on her for the fact that she still had to feed us separately. She would be forced to take small loans from others, ask help from the Sisters of Charity, and do odd jobs for people in order to make just enough money to feed us, most often without feeding herself.

Vanessa and I were so little that, even though we saw sad times, such as my mother being beaten before our very eyes, she never showed us that she was hurt or sad. She usually recovered very quickly, and would tell us things like, "I'm going to take you out to see your father; do not upset him or worry him with any of this, or I won't take you there again". For us, it was a treasured outing to be taken by my mother on the tram to see him. Despite wanting desperately to tell my father that Mum had been beaten, and even though we were finding it very hard to keep quiet about it – we constantly whispered to each other, debating whether to tell or not – we never did say a word. My father always saved his meal for us, one that Vanessa and I looked forward to and ate with great relish.

Later on in life, my father said, "I always knew that things were very, very hard for you and your mother. She's a very strong woman, but she would never let you tell me the truth. But I knew that things were not all that great." I take my hat off to her for her strength and the love she had for all of us.

Having been through a lot in our young lives already – including Dum Dum, the loss of our siblings, and being sheltered for many months under the steps – Vanessa and I were usually happy and content with what we had, and being children didn't know any different. We were skin and bone but still smiled and played and cried like other kids, and had no idea what we were severely lacking.

The man in the local restaurant always gave us these little wraps filled with savoury vegetables and herbs, or whatever else he used to make things in his shop. He would always give us one or two free, because he would be frying hundreds of them. A few broken ones that couldn't be sold didn't really matter. He loved us because we were so fair and different from the other kids, and we always stood in front of his huge vessel, staring at him with mouths wide open. I'm sure, irrespective of who he was and his background, he did have a heart, and he certainly had a lot of compassion.

Watching him had a lingering influence on us years later. Even after we moved away, when we did the dishes together Vanessa and I used to actually play the fry-cook game. I would scrub the dishes with the ash gathered from a local tea shop (like he prepared the batter) and then Vanessa would dip them in water (the way he fried them in oil). I fondly remember that role-playing game to this day. It kept us going, since we never had any toys or anything to play with, and had to make the best of what we had.

When my mother was successful at bringing us something to eat, I remember her always telling us that we should eat what she brought for us. At first we'd always hold back, saying something like, "But Mum, what about you?"

As I write this, I can still see her standing there, offering the food with one hand and waving away our concern for her with the other, saying something like, "My friend just fed me and I'm just bursting with food! I can't eat another morsel. I'm so full; I'll just have to sit down. So please, you take it...go on without me." The truth was that she had not just had a hearty meal with one of her friends, nor had she actually eaten anything at all, sometimes for days. We knew it; but were so hungry ourselves, if she said "No," we just ate it.

There were times we saw her become really weak and she would just stop to rest along the way. She would close her eyes, steady herself, and keep going about her daily chores. All this was probably because of extreme hunger. Stress, lack of food, constant beatings and really demanding physical work was beginning to show their ill effects. Her health began to deteriorate rapidly and obviously.

She didn't even have a real pair of shoes to her name. What she wore were two pieces of leather held together, and tied up with string around and around her feet. Those were the shoes she would be wearing when she had to leave us to play for the day with the children of a local hotel guard who lived nearby, and the shoes she would be wearing when she returned, tired and mostly empty-handed. The amazing thing was that I do not remember her complaining, even for one day. Although in declining health, we never saw anything of the kind from her.

My father said it was mainly his heart attack that put the pressure on her to take charge and be responsible for keeping us dry, warm, and fed. Sadly, he took quite a long time to recover, and she was left with this responsibility for much longer than she could mentally and physically manage. She bravely fought on, day after day after day.

As we continued to stay there throughout those months, it became clear that Vanessa's and my health – we were only little kids – was starting to deteriorate as well. The area under the steps was one of the worst of all miserable possibilities on earth. The foetid ditch of stagnant run-off water from the pump, which stretched, festering, across the width in front of our area, bred disease and foul odours. We were frequently very ill. This was due to many reasons, mainly near-starvation and malnourishment, sleeping where roaches and vermin came out of muddy holes in a perpetually damp flooring, and not having any stability or proper clothes to wear. All of the squalor affected our health, leading my mother to put us with a woman called Mrs Cleofas.

Jill's first home

CHAPTER SEVEN:

MRS CLEOFAS

Calcutta can be a very difficult place for little girls – especially Indian-English ones.

In the West, I have met women who have lost very young children, and then have watched them receive support and assistance from all quarters. I have great compassion for them. Yet, with the grisly image of grief etched upon my mother's heart, she had to deal with one death after another, amongst a waterfall of so many other problems. She bore all this overwhelming anguish, but with no support at all. It makes me always stop to think of her and the sure strength she had to have been able to move on like she did, horrid incident after incident, in a country where welfare just did not exist. To this very moment I still reflect on her ability to keep going, and it makes me feel by comparison that I did not have it that bad. She took the worst blows upon herself to defend us from them.

Kindness comes in many faces. The memory of my mother's face is a bouquet of these very special flowers, her gifts, her will, her determination. On the other hand, it seemed as if the woman who took care of Vanessa and me to get us away from the steps, Mrs Cleofas, had never heard of the word.

Living under the steps had proven to be too much for my mother, so she begged the old woman – who resembled an old witch, with a terrible face and worse breath – to take us in. She owned a proper house and told my mother she would look after us, and that she would teach us as well. Of course, my mother jumped at the chance.

That eccentric old woman constantly beat us and, for some reason, was always after me in particular. I remember my sister and me huddled up, living in fear of what Mrs Cleofas would do next. There were slaps, pokes, sharp sticks, spoons, and brooms, a lone knuckle popped into the side of our heads. Cruelty and our terror of it inspired Mrs Cleofas, and she used it as an instrument of 'education', like a pointer in a classroom. Mrs Cleofas taught at the end of all these weapons.

At this point, my nerves had been taxed by death, illness, and poverty, worry for my father who was ill, and my mother who was still living under the stairs. The more violent Mrs. Cleofas grew in her lessons, I, already being the nervous one, became yet more nervous. I could not concentrate on anything, and fear paralysed me. I stood motionless, waiting for the blows to land. The expected ensuing slaps and pokes were energetically and constantly dished out. I was intimidated by too many jabs and knocks, too frightened to think of an answer, let alone to offer one or to raise an arm in any form of self-defence. This, in turn, earned more kicks, slaps, pokes and beatings from our guardian.

I was perfectly normal, but she insisted that one of my eyes looked horizontally and one vertically, and that is why I was slow and unable to grasp anything. There was nothing wrong with me, other than the fear of being beaten continuously. I became even more frightened as the pinches, punches, and beatings continued.

The eccentric old woman learned quickly that I was terrified of cockroaches, especially the big ones. This revelation led to her worst atrocity toward me. Why she perpetrated this deviant routine, I will never know. She started to lock me in the toilet – her Indian-style toilet. It was half the size of a phone booth, filthy, cramped, and had a smell I cannot describe. She would first show me that the dark and ugly chamber of misery was infested with huge, flying cockroaches...hundreds of them. I used to tremble just at the thought of going in there. According to Mrs Cleofas this was where I belonged, and so in the evenings she would catch me by my ear, take me to the toilet, show me the hundreds of cockroaches and then push me in there. She would lock the door, and put off the light from the outside.

I could take any amount of beatings, tortures, and ugliness, but I would rather have died than be locked inside there. There was never a day when I came out of there without wetting myself.

I can assure you in no uncertain terms that abuses breed emotional welts that require the salve of familiar affections. I'm not sure where my mother used to stay or if she went back to the place under the steps every day, but when she visited we never got a word in. I had the feeling she knew something was not quite right because I couldn't speak a word without stuttering or trembling...but what could she do about it?

My mother was grateful to Mrs Cleofas for looking after us. She didn't imagine what was happening, and thought that it was the best place for us for the time being. When her all-too-short and infrequent visits ended, to me, it was almost unbearable to see my mother leave, because it meant I would have to endure many more sessions in the toilet. I usually ended up with a very high temperature and sobbed all night, wishing that the next day would never come.

So it was that Mrs Cleofas looked after us for quite a while, until she decided that she didn't want to any longer. She also seemed to be ageing before our very eyes, and must have felt that we were not worth the bother. By this point my mother too could no longer overlook the whole pain I felt, and knew for certain that something was terribly wrong. She decided to take us home, which was back to living under the steps. This was absolute bliss for us. The gratitude we felt at no longer be frightened, beaten or terrified is something I cannot describe, and I can assure you that I wouldn't have swapped it for the best toy in the world. I remember Vanessa and myself laughing and crying at the same time the day my mother said, "Pack your things – we're leaving."

On the day we left Mrs Cleofas, I was so excited to return to under the steps that I developed a high temperature with the excitement, in the same way that normal kids develop temperatures days before they leave for Disneyland or receive an extra-special surprise. Though the place under the stairs was dark, cold, wet, and dismal, it seemed like a paradise when compared to living with that old lady and the fear of the cockroaches.

Although it was a very long walk home, which ordinarily would completely tire out a little one, I remember skipping all the way home with sheer joy while teasing back and forth the whole time with Vanessa. Our mother just gazed fondly at us, so glad to see us so happy. She knew that we had endured a lot and she did the best she could to help us at the time. She frequently smiled at us and laughed when we made up songs about Mrs Cleofas, but never failed to caution us, telling us "No matter what, we need to be grateful to her for having fed you and kept you, and let's not forget that."

Later in life, when I might have been eleven or twelve, I used to go to the aged home every week to visit the old people, a passion with which I was born. I would take them whatever I could. Vanessa and I saved our pocket money, which was only one or two rupees every week if mother could afford it. With whatever we had collected, we would buy biscuits, bread, medicine, and, if we had enough, sometimes jam. The primary thought was to give to those who never had anything at all. Never worrying about ourselves, we delighted in sharing it among the aged. It was always the highlight of our week or month. When we arrived, we always found them to have been looking out for us, since most of them never ever had any other visitors at all.

At one point we learned that Mrs Cleofas was living in the same home. When we visited her, she seemed twice as withered and mentally unstable as when we last had seen her. I remember going to her and sitting there with her. Occasionally, Vanessa cautioned me to leave her alone, concerned that she might still be quite cruel – but we had sympathy for her, and, oddly, for whatever reason, we loved her.

We felt grateful to her, because we could now understand that behind all the cruelty and beatings, she was one of the few people to have extended a helping hand to my mother and to us. Her behaviour, I understand today, might have had a lot to do with her past in some way. We spent much time with her, and never did we have even the slightest feeling of hatred for her. We danced about and adored her, taking care of her and the others. We would read to her, wipe her down, hug her, comb her hair and kiss her. Funnily enough, the sad memories just never got in the way of how we cared for her. We were happy to see her and none of those bad thoughts came in the way of the love and gratitude we felt for her.

She did not remember us, because she was very old by then. I am sure, however, that she must have done something good at some point in her life, because when nobody wanted her, our visits and kindness brought the old woman a lot of joy. Sometimes she used to hold onto our hands and fall asleep.

We never moved so as to not to disturb her. I did not know what she felt at the time, or if she recognised us at all, or knew somehow that the two little girls at her bedside were us. Yet just to be given the opportunity to thank her for everything she did for us, before she passed away, meant the world to us. If for no other reason, perhaps I felt this way only because I remember my mother instilling this almost instinctive type of response in us. Sometimes we would be given a sweet from some kind person. But if we did not say thank you, or rushed away with excitement, we would have to return and hand the sweet right back. No amount of apologies or thanks would earn us that sweet back. The words "thank you" and "I'm sorry" have been instilled in us since birth.

If I think about it now, it is clear that Mrs Cleofas did take some of her own frustrations out on us, and I can never forget the wretched, claustrophobic, cockroach-infested toilet where she had locked me in, saying it was where I belonged. But somewhere, somehow, sometime, she had managed to touch both my sister and me in many small ways. If nothing else, I will remain forever grateful to her for relieving some of the stress my mother felt about the sad and dangerous state of our family's affairs.

CHAPTER EIGHT:
KIDDERPORE. SIX PEOPLE, ONE ROOM & A TINY VERANDA

At last, after more than eight months at the Salvation Army, my father got better. Having been such a long time, my mother, Vanessa and I were overjoyed to see him up and about, vigorous and back to his old self, like he was during the early days at Dum Dum. We had all been through a lot; he in convalescence, and we under the thumbs of Mrs Cleofas and the two landladies above the stairs.

He moved us to a local hotel called Berus Lodge until we could find a house, which was proving to be nearly impossible because of the deposits and guarantees one had to pay in order to rent one. We stayed in the hotel and my father joined Dunlop PLC in the administration department. As he began to earn some money, my parents kept looking for a house, since the hotel – even though the cheapest in the area and in a terrible condition – was not affordable for any length of time. Calling it a hotel, in fact, is being copiously generous, as the place was little more than a shelter where the poor stayed. They were small, cramped rooms with leaking walls, one pull-down bed, one light bulb and one wooden stool for a table.

It was then that he came home one evening and started spitting blood. My mother once again came to the rescue. Just by giving him water, making him lie down, sending me to the pharmacy to buy some tablets, rubbing him down and praying, she saved his life. We later called a local physician, Dr Sinha, who tended to my father and didn't charge us at all. Once again, as we learnt later, he had had a minor cardiac arrest.

Then, a few days after the scare with my father, we learnt that Mr Nazareth had passed away. It was as though the entire world was crashing down on us. Once again, my mother had no one to turn to. This news was devastating to all of us. Mr Nazareth was the man who had never failed to come to our aid at all times – and we had lost him, too.

My father got better, took an advance from work, and rented one small room in Kidderpore, which is a very poor area in the far southwest of Calcutta. Settling us closer to the school where my sisters were, the rent was sixty rupees per month (approximately seventy pence per month), yet it was a sum that my father was still unable to pay. The Landlord threatened to throw us out on many an occasion, because we owed two years' rent. The rent arrears lingered a long time, primarily because my father had borrowed 500 rupees (approximately 8 pounds) and had to pay interest every month on that amount. Until the day my mother died, we were still unable to clear the debt or pay the rent. It was a single room with a little veranda and situated in an extremely narrow passageway, barely wide enough for one person to walk through.

As one faced the entry door, ours was the second room on the right in a line of six little rooms. When you entered the passageway, on your right were three public bathrooms. which were shared by more than fifteen hundred people or more. Never cleaned, infested with cockroaches, lizards and rats, they had no flushes and smelt like nothing on earth. To the left was a cleared area with a tube well that serviced the thousands of people who used the toilets in the area.

It was a house. And it was ours. And we were overjoyed to be there. It meant stability for us, and a place that we could at long last call home. At least, it was at first.

The room was ten feet by six feet, with the floor cracked right across. From those cracks, all kinds of insects, rats and centipedes used to come out of the ground, mostly at night. My mother tried to seal it in with mud and other materials, but they always reappeared. All that fitted inside was a bed and a chair, a tin and two small tables that were placed along three walls of the room. All were arranged against the side of the walls, which were covered in vermin, an unsurprising situation, given the state of the slum and the facilities it provided. Although we got rid of a lot of them, still no matter how hard we tried to eliminate them, they simply never went away.

The veranda was ten feet by four feet. In it we had three buckets of water, a stove, a small coal-burning mud oven, and a few bricks to keep the drain water from getting into the house. It usually happened anyway, since the drain ran along the front of the house. It was only ten inches wide and approximately six inches deep, and was used by almost 300 families.

A lady would come by every three to four days to clean out the drain. She would pick up everything with either a little piece of tin or her bare hands, putting it all in a bucket. Then she took it away, needing only but a few steps to throw it onto a huge dustbin across the road from where we lived. You could get the smell of it from ten miles away. Crawling with rats, dozens of other vermin and a billion flies, that heap was where people threw all their waste on a daily basis. They also used it as a public toilet. Local people used to feed their pigs there and then sell the meat to those who lived nearby.

What can I say? It was worse than terrible. Having no money, most often no power at all, and being abused at every given opportunity – all at the same time – was just something else. I'm really not sure how we survived it, but this little room was home to us. For whatever reasons, it was most important to be together. Finally living in one place as a family unit did bring a degree of happiness and stability into our lives. The tiny miracle we experienced was that we no longer needed to be separated from each other. My mother was not being beaten. We children were not being beaten. The family felt a reinforced ability to face it all that we did not hold on to when separated.

Over time, conditions there have actually grown much worse. The last time I went back, it struck me as unbelievable how much the place has deteriorated now. Sadly, despite the rise of a prosperous middle class in India, things over there simply don't get any better for people who are like we were – the poorest of the poor. They just get worse by the year.

Over time we settled in, and my father continued with his job. The primary earner in the family, come rain, hail, storm or sickness, he got up every morning and went to work. My mother looked after us and took in small tuitions, teaching English to young children from the neighbourhood. It did not earn her very much, but it meant that she could stay home to look after Vanessa and me.

By the time my brother Neil was born in 1978 my mother had grown very tired, very fragile, and couldn't cope with much more. She gave birth to him in a free local hospital and was sent home the same day. The hospital was a terrible, awful place, where the circumstances were unbelievably wretched. It was disgusting even just to see its squalor, but that's where she gave birth. When Neil was brought home, it became obvious to us that my mother loved him so very much.

While recovering at the Salvation Army, my father had resourcefully taught himself shorthand. As luck would have it, the new skill enabled him to change jobs, and he joined a law firm called L.S Davar and Company as a stenographer, since getting any other job at his age was proving to be impossible. In a significant way, his learning this trade saved our lives. I'm sure it could not have been easy to go from a senior officer in the army to a stenographer, but the important part is that he did what he had to do in order to help us all survive.

By the time my father had joined the firm, Vanessa and myself were old enough to be admitted to the same

73

boarding school where my elder sisters were, because it was quite close to our house and was free. The school cared for us all and provided us a foundation that has sustained us all our lives. Truly, the place was our first real home, and we were saved from a lot of the dangers of 'what could have been' just by being admitted to it.

Our school and community produced some of the best athletes in the city and the country, my own sisters and cousin topping the charts on that one. Our sports teacher put on some of the best drill displays that the city had ever seen. Our drama teachers put on some of the best plays people had ever witnessed, like My Fair Lady, The Wedding Breakfast, Annie, and so on. Furthermore, some of the best singers and performers were turned out from among us, as well.

Most of these people, I might add, happened to be Indian-English, more commonly known as Anglo-Indians today. Many were extremely talented and very creative, and after the sound education that the school provided, managed to find jobs abroad, although still many others got left behind. I remember watching The Sound Of Music in a London theatre. It took me back to the teachers and students who presented plays in my school; to those who represented the community, and yet got left behind, all for want of an opportunity.

Our community really did turn out talent: singers, dancers, athletes and artists, not to mention some of the most beautiful girls in the world, if only some of them were given an opportunity to pursue better careers for themselves. We were inspired, and were taught to inspire the generations below us. We were taught with music, for example the ABBA song 'I had a dream'. These words, I understand today, were what shaped our lives for the better. Given everything most of us had gone through, our community still continued to see something good in everything! However, the talent that our people possessed never left the boundaries of the school, and on most occasions was overlooked. Life began after school, and with it came extreme hardship and the need to survive, meaning that any potential for pursuing talent had to give way to the necessity of finding even a meagre source of income straight away. Many of our girls were pursued by rich men because of their beauty and difference in looks and personality, and most often settled for relationships that either harmed them or hurt them, for one reason alone; to survive.

No work meant no food. So the choice was made for us. The talent got wrapped up and put away – a treasured journal of one's youth. In those days, India was not a country that boosted these talents. For example, many kids from our community possessed extraordinary abilities in sports. Yet, sadly enough, if they were not very academically-minded, they got left behind. Many kids had extraordinary singing talents but, because they could not sing in the local language, they were not given as much as a second glance.

Whereas home was a sad and unhealthy place to be, we fared better by remaining at school, because there we had the opportunity to give our best and prove ourselves. At the same time, we also suffered some very sad times in school. We were very poor and, unlike many of the children we were surrounded by, all we got was board, lodge and an education. For everything else, we just had to look on. As children, we found it hard to accept why other kids around us could buy and eat cakes and biscuits from the canteen and we couldn't. It hurt. I remember myself and Vanessa hanging around some kids and picking up the wrapper of a cake or biscuit, picking off the morsels and eating them. I remember it tasting so good.

My sister and I hatched more schemes for remedying the problem. We would wait for break time on a school day, and then follow the day-scholar students around.

They were the ones who came to school only for the day, and would bring their lunch or tiffin with them. We would walk round and round, searching the dry school drains for a sweet, half an eaten sandwich, or any other thing that was edible and that we could get to. This sometimes meant that we had to crawl into the covered ends of the drain, pretending that we had dropped a pencil or rubber in, and we would come out with a piece of food. We would then run to the toilet and either wash the sweet morsel under the tap and share it, or brush off the dust from a portion of a sandwich and take one bite each.

Being so young, we missed our home and my mother and father terribly. Thankfully, my father's new job made it possible for him to afford to have us for a visit every now and then. The most joyful occasion that existed, the very highlight of our days, was seeing our parents again. Its specialness stood in its own light, even though it meant going back to complete destitution, abject poverty, a life swimming in squalor – no electricity, no proper drinking water, and encounters with men from every angle.

Being home meant helping with the housework, seeing our little brother, and helping with the cooking. Although our time was filled mostly with more hardship and pain, with hardly ever a thought of an outing to a park or a funfair or to a birthday party, we didn't mind a bit. Just to be there was so fulfilling. Truly amazing were the times, on our birthdays, when we could be taken on an outing to the local zoo with a picnic basket. It only cost one rupee to get in, and, for us, that was a dream come true. The thought of going to the zoo was so exciting that I sometimes developed a fever from the anticipation, sometimes leading to the trip being called off – which, of course, made me unpopular around the house for the next few days.

I still recall times in that little room, such as the fun we had every morning when Dad played music like My coat of many colours, A Pink Toothbrush and a Blue Toothbrush, Bimbo, Blanket on the Ground, 57 Chevrolet, Chicken Every Sunday and so on from an old, broken-down tape recorder that he had got from somewhere. No matter the amount of privation, he would try to put on a brave face and make us as happy as he could while we were at home. He would tickle us, tease us and make up songs, like, Back to school you go, back to school you go, back to see mother Everesly (who was one of our much loved matrons), and back to school you go!

We dreaded songs like that one, because it meant that we had to go back to boarding school, which led us to worrying about our parents and how they might manage to find the strength to carry on. We knew they were suffering – impoverished, with their health breaking down, burdened with financial difficulties, and living in total poverty. We almost felt guilty about having food to eat and a clean place to stay in boarding school. But, leaving our hearts with them at home, we had to go back to school. Regardless of how dire the circumstances were there, we would cry, fight, show temper, beg and promise to do whatever my mother asked, just to go home for a day or two. We wanted to be home, and to help in any way we could.

Who knows what would have become of us children without that beacon of light provided by our boarding school to sustain our lives? For that, I shall be forever grateful to my parents for always maintaining that we go back to school and get an education. Sometimes we would feel scared because our teachers or matrons asked us to bring in something like thread for a needlework class, or ink, or polish, or even toothpaste. My parents couldn't afford any of those things, but they still put us back to school without it, knowing that we would manage somehow.

We got punished, but most of the time the teachers and

matrons understood the reason behind us not being able to bring in what was asked of us, and kindly let us off the hook or found a way to give it to us. Being in a boarding school, we soon learnt to stand up for ourselves, to fight back and become little leaders, so to speak. There were always kids who used to love us for teaching them English or for allowing them to be part of our group.

We soon became the popular ones, being Indian-English. We frequently received a lot of free things from the school. Later we learnt the gifts were sent for us by our sponsors, the people living abroad whom the school contacted, and who graciously paid for our education. The school seldom identified them to us, even though they made us write and re-write thank you letters which we'd hand to the matrons, who posted them on our behalf. Sometimes our sponsors visited the school and met with us in person.

Every now and again, a little extra money was given to us for a school fete or some such occasion for us to spend it on. It wasn't very much at all, but since we hardly ever received any pocket money, to us it meant a great deal. Some sponsors would also approach the school in order to adopt children. There were many times when my mother was approached with these offers, but she always refused to give any of us up.

There were a few who wrote to her especially asking to adopt us, because of the way we looked. Rising to the occasion, she never hesitated to berate the school authorities, saying, "I am grateful for the help, but I don't need it if they want my children in return." She always said, "We might be poor, we might not have any worldly goods; but I do love my children, and no amount of money in the world can part me from them or part them from each other."

I remember the year it rained continuously for over two weeks. It caused deadly flash floods that brought the whole city to a complete standstill. With poor to virtually non-existent drainage, and no proper sanitary arrangements, diseases ran rampant. While we were relatively safe and dry in school, people were going around in upturned beds, using them as boats, and – at huge premiums – selling bread, vegetables, or any foodstuffs they could muster, at inflated rates.

My school shut down and our principal allowed all the poor people to come in and live in our classrooms. We were not allowed out of the dormitories, but could watch the people flowing in and crowding into every block in the school.

For us, it was fun to be off school, but over many long periods during the crisis, my little sister and I spent our time anxiously looking out of the windows from our dormitory, hoping for a glimpse of someone that had rescued Mum, Dad and our little brother, and would bring them to safety. My elder sister Donna, who lived in central Calcutta, tried to pay a taxi double the amount of money to fetch my parents or to drop them some food, but he refused. There were no phones or means of communication. They were completely cut off from the rest of the world. But we never saw them. We were too little to understand the full extent of the problem, but I remember knowing that there was something terribly wrong. Later, we came to know what really had happened.

After many weeks and the floods had subsided, we finally saw my mother at school. She had come to see us and had brought my little brother with her. We sobbed our hearts out upon seeing her. They looked so thin, and literally starving; hungry, dirty, and worn out. Yet, when they saw us, their smiles were unforgettable. At that moment, we wanted nothing more than to hug them and know that they were all right.

Eventually, after some pestering, my mother, with grave reluctance, revealed to us what had happened. The floods rose up into the area of our one-room home, which had almost no sanitary provisions whatsoever. Inescapably, with the flooding water continuing to rise, everything in the area was under water. There was no leeway because that narrow passage with a huge building less than three feet away acted as a funnel, flushing torrents directly past the front of our house. Everything was full of water.

It then started to fill up the little room that my parents and my little brother Neil were in. There she sat, with a baby in her arms and my father at her side, deliriously waiting for the water to subside. For days they prayed that the rain would stop and that the little room would not fill up any more. They had lifted the bed on its side and had sat on the top edge, with no electricity, no food, and everything soaked or floating around them, while the water kept rising.

When she told us how my parents and my little brother were in that room, seated on the bed for days, I cried inconsolably. The terrible feeling overcame us that we could have lost them; they could have drowned in that one room. After everything we had been through, this episode just traumatised us as we imagined what might have happened. They might have been washed away and thrown onto piles with a thousand other bodies. Would my mother have left Neil on the top shelf that was almost near the roof in that little room, on which only a little one could fit, before she died, hoping that the waters would recede and that someone would find him? We might never have known what had happened to them, or even found Neil at all.

My mother said that most people in our area had been rescued, but my father refused to go, because he never thought for a moment that things would get so serious. Given the choice of being at home, they could avoid the degradation and crowding, which came from living with hundreds of others in the makeshift areas that were made available for flood victims. He was a very proud man and had his dignity, but I'm sure he didn't realise just how extreme things would become. If the rain had persisted much longer, they surely would have met the most horrifying deaths ever. I still had nightmares about this, years later, and can't think of this tragic scene without getting terribly upset. I guess it is because I was unable to deal with another loss. It was something that just could not be accepted in my mind.

Eventually the rains stopped and the water receded, leaving devastation and even greater poverty in its wake.

My mother believes it was her prayers that saved them. People spent months cleaning up the school and the area, trying desperately to bring it back to normal.

When my mother came to see us in boarding school she had nothing to give us, but that didn't matter at all. All the other girls were eating and buying things, but we didn't ask for anything or want anything. We just wanted to hold them and ask about every detail that happened. I'm sure that things were much worse than my mother made them out to be. As usual, she did not want to worry us.

Instead, we spent those days locked up in our dormitories, traumatised that the building we lived in was already under water and that our parents were huddled together with the other poor people, starving, praying for the rain to stop. The hardest thing in the world is to want to be with the people you love, when all the while you're locked up against your will.

The most telling moment came when visiting hours were over, as we watched her pick up my little brother and walk across the field towards the school gate. Absolutely exhausted, skin and bones really, but making out to us that she was fine and was invited to a friend's house for dinner, she trudged away in the mud. We knew that not only did she have to walk all the way home carrying my baby brother in her arms but she was also going back to nothing. We stood there and watched her walk out of sight, knowing that we would soon go in to have dinner provided by the school.

It was those thoughts that killed us inside, those thoughts that hurt so badly. It is impossible to describe – that feeling of not being able to do anything, just desperately, achingly, wanting to be with her, or to help her, knowing that they had nothing to eat and were walking all the way home. But she would have none of it. She made us stay in school, where she knew we would be sheltered, fed, and kept warm.

I have, until this day, never met a woman so strong and so astoundingly courageous. It fills me with tremendous pride and gratitude to realise that, above all, that amazing tower of strength was my mother.

Jill's second home

CHAPTER NINE:
POOR KIDS IN KIDDERPORE

Kidderpore is where most of the saddest part of our lives took place. Into our ramshackle environment, my parents delivered their last child, Susan. Around the time she was born, two years after Neil, everything started boiling up, yet again, and circumstances seemed to collapse in upon us once more. Come to think of it, it should probably have been clear from the time we moved in that this was not the area we were supposed to be in. It was not a place for us in which to flourish or thrive.

I can tell you that, even though we loved to be home, it was also terrible, too. We took any opportunity to be able to see our parents and our little brother, even if we didn't have our own bedroom or bed and had to sleep on the floor, or we'd be lucky to have one meal a day. We were just happy to be there – to see my parents, to hug them, and to sit with them, before we were put back again away from them for long periods of time.

I was ten years old and home for the holidays, waiting for the new baby to be born and brought from the hospital.

As was the case most of the time, there was no electricity, and it was extremely humid and frightfully hot. We were sweating bucket-loads and I remember having quite a few boils because of the heat. Vanessa's little body was red with prickly heat. The room was equivalent to a dungeon – absolutely dark, with bare necessities and a furnace, to be honest

Even before she had Neil, the doctors had already repeatedly warned my mother that she shouldn't have any more children, and that if she did, there was little or no chance of them surviving. They also warned her about the risk of her own survival if there was another birth. Despite the warnings, Susan was born. Sadly, by then my mother's health had noticeably deteriorated, to the point where she herself was not expected to live.

My elder sister Donna, who was trying to make something of her own life, used to help as and when she could. My younger sister Vanessa came home from school during one break and her little heart broke to see us struggling, sick, and starving – yet, we were together. As little as she was, she refused to go back to school. She wanted to stay and help me, even more because the new baby was expected. Barely able to manage to cope with everything, I was happy to have someone my age I could depend on to support me, and someone with whom I could share my troubles with. Together we ran the house. We looked after and bathed Neil and the newborn baby, looked after them, cooked, did all the chores, ran to the shops, and did whatever was necessary to keep the house alive.

After three days, my mother brought Susan home. When she arrived, she told us the doctor had directed her to take the baby home. They had done everything they could for her, and to save the baby. They wanted the family to spend time with the child, but clearly the newborn was not going to survive.

My parents had lost four children and had dealt with unimaginable hardship. Now, to be told that Susan wasn't expected to live, was more than they could handle. The pain was too much to bear and impossible to comprehend. I now know that people deal with such situations in strange manners in order to try and separate themselves from the pain, and my mother was no exception to the rule.

My mother got home and put Susan on the bed, and related more of what the doctor had advised her – that the child was going to die in a few days, and to let the family spend the last days with her. My mother spoke in a tone that was heartbreaking, as if to say, "I have lost my other little ones, and this is going to happen again," with an expression of such sadness and hurt. I shall never forget it.

When I looked at Susan and shook her head, I actually thought that she was dead already. She was a baby who was born with rickets (rachitis), weakening of the bones caused by deficiency of vitamin D, calcium, or phosphate – or all three. With eyes seemingly right out of their sockets, lost at the back of her head, and an extremely swollen belly with limbs as thin as matchsticks, her hands stuck out like spindles, like knitting needles.

I didn't care what she looked like or anything. I knew she was sick and I heard my mother tell us what the doctor said but, in a way, I heard nothing. All I knew is that she was part of me and I couldn't let her go. I don't know why, but I loved her instantly. It was the same way in which my sister Donna loved the twins, Kimberley and Alan. I just loved Susan.

As we stood by the bed, my mother said, "She's going to die, so let's all just be around her. The doctor's given us these medicines." Given free by hospitals to virtually-dying children and very poor people, the medicines were just powders wrapped up in white pieces of paper like homeopathic medicine, but were not, in fact, homeopathic.

They were just white powders wrapped up and put in an envelope, then handed to people who couldn't afford to buy proper medicines.

My mother was extremely tired, in very poor health. She was finished with her life, so to speak, and had been forced, against the truest power of will, to give up almost entirely. Very weak from the delivery, she couldn't go on another day, and didn't have anything left to give the baby anyway. Beyond the slightest question or slimmest hint of a doubt, she had been through a lot. Helpless against the tidal wave of afflictions that beset us, everything had, in a way, taken its toll on her. She was simply exhausted, broken, and at the end of the line. I wanted to try and do all I could to make my mother happy. I knew that if this child could be saved, it would give her a little hope to go on, and I was going to try to do my best for the family. I had no idea how I was going to accomplish anything, but I knew that our love would save her.

My father said, "Well, Susan's going to die. That's fine...we know that. But she is still here with us now. Let's do everything we can to make her comfortable, and show her that she was blessed. She has been sent to our family for a reason and, for however short a period of time, we need to show her a lot of love and care."

I remember Neil, a two-year-old with such a cute face, standing there, totally unaware that his little sister was dying. He couldn't stop staring at her and touching her terribly thin fingers, not wanting to stop kissing her. I seized upon this idea, and asked Mum, "How are we supposed to give her the medicine?"

She answered, "Well, you have to give her the medicine every half an hour, and I don't know how the doctor expects me to do it. He's a madman." Still, she went on to my father, "We need to mix it with Electral (which is glucose) or milk, and give her this syrup every half hour. Just add one powder after mixing it with water, and give it to her."

We had no milk, so I went to the local teashop asking for credit, explaining that we had a new baby at home. A man named Ashok gave me a bowl of milk, which was 80% water. I saw him empty one jug of milk into a big vessel and then add at least three jugs of water to it. I didn't care, only because I was extremely grateful, since he didn't change me for the milk – he just filled up my bowl. I brought it home and started feeding spoonfuls to her drop by drop, mixing the powders in every half hour.

Most of the time, my mother went to the Sisters of Charity and brought home some milk, sugar, clothes, biscuits, etc. When that finished, I used to leave Vanessa, who was eight years old at the time, to take care of Susan while I ran to the Sisters of Charity. I lined up with all the other poor people to whom they give powdered milk in plastic bags. Everyone got one bag of milk, one packet of biscuits and a plastic bag of clothes. So I collected that, came home, mixed up the milk and continued giving it to Susan. Even though Neil was just two years old at the time and longed for a little milk, we used to ensure that he didn't get any, because the baby in the house need it much more than him.

We had a little rusted alarm clock that made a loud noise, startling me and leaving a ringing in my ears every time it went off. The excellence of it though was that it would just jolt me awake and I could hurry to give her the medicine. I prayed and prayed over her. I sponged her and kissed her, I cried for her and stared at her. Throughout every day and night, I set that alarm clock every half hour to alert me, and I gave her the medicine with some water in a glass. I just kept pressing her cheeks (like a butterfly flower) and kept putting it down her throat every time with a teaspoon.

I can still see in my mind's eye the sorrowful vision of my mother speaking to people, saying the doctor told her that the baby wasn't expected to live; that even if she did survive, she might have been severely handicapped, and that we would know in a few weeks or months to come. Even though many didn't actually say it, they thought it would be better if God took her. During that very sad and depressing time, living in a cramped dingy house and waiting for the moment for death to arrive was beyond imagination.

I cried my heart out every time I was left alone and in charge, and Susan didn't respond. I always thought she was dead, and used to live in fear – not that I did anything wrong, but just the thought of losing her was something I couldn't bear, so I kept up the medicine for weeks on end. Loving her more than my very self, I continued to watch over her; wiping her down, fanning her because we had no electricity, but most of all just loving and praying for her, until a miracle happened. And it did. I do believe that the power of intention does work, even though most people do not realise it. After studying the subject, I believe in it one hundred percent, and now teach it at all my training courses.

Slowly, she started to respond. She came to life. She survived. Words fail to describe what profound and significant joy I felt when I saw that I had nursed her back to health.

She definitely was not expected to live long, but were she to persist it was suggested that it would take years to get her to any semblance of true health. Despite being unable to walk or talk until very late in childhood, she made it. I've looked after her ever since, and if you meet her today you wouldn't believe she was that little baby. She was chosen as School Captain, topped her university in the UK, and besides being extremely beautiful and highly intelligent, she is a person of exceptional qualities as well.

During this very same period of time, I was also looking after my brother, only two years old himself. What's worse is that my mother's health deteriorated even more. She was too weak to care and too sick and disillusioned to even try to help. As I was the oldest child in the house at the time she would deflect any ministrations from me, and told me to look after the little ones, Neil and Susan.

In this manner, having looked after Neil since he was born, after Susan's arrival I became the eight-year-old virtual Mum. Over time, I even had to take that role in reality. I cared for my younger siblings because my mother was incapacitated. I could have actually died there on many an occasion, along with Vanessa, Neil and Susan. It reminds me of the movie Flowers in the Attic – except that we were four little flowers, in a place probably worse than the Black Hole of Calcutta!

My mother had no option but to keep me out of school, and informed the school authorities that I was very sick with chicken pox. Actually, of course, I stayed to look after the little ones. When at last she got a bit better, she started going out to central Calcutta in search of help, food, or anything she could manage to pull together.

I was there throughout this period, bringing up both children with Vanessa at my side, freeing up my mother's time to try and get some money and anything else we so desperately needed. I remember one year Mum didn't put me to school for about eight months. She just kept me home to look after the children while she went about trying to earn or secure some money, doing odd jobs here and there. She was forced into it by our circumstances. My dad wasn't earning enough to support us, due to the added burden of two starving children and a very sick child. When the increased rent of eighty rupees proved impossible to pay, the landlord started to harass us. He abused us, locked us out of our house, abused my mother, kicked our buckets of water over, spat in our house, and more.

When I used to kiss my father goodbye just before he left for work, he would always tell me, "Hold the fort. We all have our crosses to carry, and ours are much lighter than what others in the world have been given. Carry it with pride, and remember that there is a reason for everything that happens in life." I was afraid that he was struggling mightily, too, and, when he eventually had his third heart attack, he had to go and live with a friend in the city in order to get better and survive. He lost his job, which put even more pressure on us.

Sometimes my mother would be out from early morning until late at night, leaving us with just very little or no money at all to manage for food. There were no phones in case anything went wrong with the little ones, and there was no place that we could contact her or knew where she had gone. She pretended to make social visits to better-off friends she had, so that she could pack up the food they offered her and bring it home for us. Mr Neil O'Brien – who was on several Boards of Education including our school board, was a member of Parliament, and who helped hundreds of families to survive and to make something of themselves – used to help my mother tremendously. He felt that she was an extraordinary person, and that we were blessed to have her as our mother. His wife, too, loved my mother, and helped our family tremendously.

Some of the time her friends would make her have a meal, and would also pack a little food and send it for us. At other times she would have borrowed money to buy something on the way, or stopped by the meat man (butcher) to take twenty-five grams of meat on credit. She pawned the little transistor radio we had for twenty rupees (twenty-five pence) to a man who sold vegetables, in order to pay other bills and to conjure a tiny meal out of it.

I couldn't understand it at that time. All I knew was that they were my parents and I loved them dearly, along with the two little ones, my siblings and Vanessa, who meant the world to me. I never thought of tomorrow or the day after; we lived by the day. We never knew then that children our age had proper lives that differed from ours, but such ignorance was bliss for us. Happy to be merely there for each other, we simply didn't know any better. We were left in God's hands, and we survived.

In the late evenings we put the little ones to sleep, and Vanessa and I went to the local teashop and waited until the night, when the merchant had put out the huge fire in the clay oven. Then we would dig the hot ashes out of the coal fire pit with a stick and bring them home to clean our dishes with.

We washed loads of laundry at the tube-well. I remember my father's pants being so big that we had to hold the clothes-washing brush in our hands while running up and down his trousers, like the little mice in the movie Cinderella trying to wash something three times our size. We would take hold of the garment on both sides, then squeeze and squeeze with all our might. All this failed to accomplish the task because, as we were too weak to wring enough of the water out of it, it was still too heavy to lift and hang it up to dry.

We washed the dishes with dried leaves and ash because we couldn't afford soap or washing powder. Vanessa and I would make a game out of it, having competitions to see who could make their dishes shine brighter. Our little hands sometimes bled from the rigorous scrubbing and sometimes got burnt from the hot ash that we picked up from the oven, but we just moved on and didn't let anything dampen our spirits.

Starving most days, occasionally we danced for local men in exchange for food, or we went to ask for a cup of tea on credit. Frequently reduced to just sitting and crying with hunger while holding the little ones, who were crying, too, we waited until midnight, praying that my mother was okay and might come home with something to eat.

Our landlord used to make my sister and me dance their local dances. Then he'd buy us a corn on the cob each, but not without trying to touch us, and this was only because there was no one to look after us. My mother had gone out in search of work, food or money, and my father had gone to work too. We didn't understand them wanting to touch us, so long as we got some sweets, a Coca-Cola to share, corn on the cob, or anything else out of the deal. Being children and hungry most of the time, left unattended, we didn't mind dancing a bit more – and if it meant getting something to eat in return, well then, so be it.

Many times all we heard was, "Hey, white rat! Come here and dance for us!" or even worse suggestions. We had several men wanting to behave inappropriately with us on any given day. We were hungry, we were alone, and we didn't understand how mean they actually were to us. Did they clap because they were depraved, or did they actually like us? We had no idea at the time, but we did what we had to do in order to survive.

I often used to ask my father as to why men would continue to abuse us and why everyone called us white rats, white lizards, white cockroaches, white slime, and all the rest. My father always answered, "What you need to remember is that our destiny should not be preordained by the colour of our skin or the country we come from...but unfortunately, in the fickle world we live in, it has a huge influence over various outcomes. You need to rise above that. That's what strength is all about. People say and do things in ignorance. Believing it or accepting it and allowing it to influence your future makes you ignorant, too; you need to make that decision."

Partly it was because the area was crawling with men, all who were extremely poor and completely illiterate. They probably didn't understand the effect this behaviour would have on a young mind. Even though both of us endured this abuse, Vanessa endured it to the greater extent since she was the fairest, and therefore it was easier for them to target her. Since it was always extremely hot and humid, it became natural to hardly have any clothes on except our panties, which were usually received from the Sisters of Charity. Most often adult knickers, they started around our waist and ended at our knees or below. Barely dressed in this way, with our fair bodies; we were, in a way, easy targets as well.

We used to fill plastic buckets with water from a hand-pump, which was quite a distance away. We had to walk in ankle-deep mud, which usually proved to be very slippery even though we were barefoot. The buckets of water and the wet laundry we'd often be carrying was too much to keep our little feet stable. On the way back home, we almost always fell and had to go back to refill the buckets and re-rinse the clothes. Sometimes crying, sometimes bleeding, sometimes laughing, and sometimes just plain angry. Nevertheless, through it all we used to get each other out of such situations and just carry on. Day after day, week after week, month after month and year after year.

Later, a pump installed closer to home helped, but it had only a very small area around it where men came to bathe, women came to wash clothes, and children used it as a toilet. We slipped many a time into the drain – bucket, clothes, utensils and all – and did get hurt. But on most occasions there wasn't time to cry about it or worry about it, only because there were two little ones who depended on us. You had to stand up and act strong, whether you liked it or not, or else they would start crying and get upset, too.

I remember once cooking stew and rice into which I had put a whole lot of effort. I started cooking the dish in the afternoon and finished the meal at around ten pm at night, on a very tiny stove. The three younger ones could not wait to start eating and kept asking me if the food was ready. Overtired and totally exhausted with the chores of the day, I picked up the aluminium pot of hot stew, holding it with both hands using a piece of cloth, and walked in from the veranda to the room – and then dropped it all on myself.

This was easily one of the saddest moments I faced during this entire episode in our lives. I saw their faces literally go into grief because they were so hungry. Not having had a proper meal in a long time, they had waited virtually all day for it to get ready...and I had dropped it!

Believe it or not, I didn't care how burnt I was, or how bad I felt. We started to pick it up, and then I cleaned the floor. We all still sat and ate it without a care in the world, and kept some for Mum, too. That is what starvation can do to you! I remember later that night sobbing about it out of sheer exhaustion, while my sister Vanessa blew on my burns and put on some cream, trying to calm me down till Mum got home.

There was once an unforgettable experience when both my sister and I were washing clothes at the tube-pump. We were carrying water back home, when Vanessa fell into a huge deep sewer. It was common for sewer covers to be left open while the sewers were being cleaned. Being very little, she fell in.

At that moment my heart stopped. Her little hand was slipping off the side where she was holding on. There was slime all over, and all sides of the manhole were covered in cockroaches and vermin. Even though I was mortally terrified of cockroaches, I didn't actually notice them. What I was unwaveringly focused on was my sister in front of my very eyes, terrified that she was going to slip away.

Thoughts surged through my mind like daggers. I could try to grab her, but feared I might not have been able to hold on to her. If that were to have happened I would have never been able to forgive myself. If I were the one who let her slip, I would have jumped to my own death after her – of that, I was sure.

Her extremely white face was a horrid picture of fear and trauma. I do not know how she managed to continue to hold on, because the manhole was so big compared to her. It was amazing that she didn't just fall straight in, never to be seen again.

I screamed to my father, and he came running. Our room was barely six steps from the manhole. He rushed over, grabbed her, and pulled her out. She came out covered in human excreta and dirt, black and blue with scrapes and grazes. We gave her a bath and put her to bed, and I remember that I cried all day. This nightmarish incident has left neither one of us. There has been many a time when I have tortured myself, thinking What if she couldn't have held on any longer? What if she had let go?

Much later on, Susan had an accident, too. One of my mother's friends gave her an old broken tricycle for the two little ones to share, and they used to play on it with some of the neighbour's children who came from Orissa (a state in India). Since there were no parks or any other possible place to play, whenever they could they'd run or take turns cycling up and down that little narrow passage, up and down, falling and getting up for long hours at a time.

One day, wearing only a little frock, my sister ran the bike to the fifth house in the row. By the door, their mother was boiling a huge pot of water on a clay oven filled with hot coals. One of the children pushed Susan in their excitement. She collided with the hot pot, which fell over, whereupon she promptly landed on the coals and the hot water. We were in our room, and had no idea of what had happened.

The lady promptly got her up and pushed her out of their veranda on her cycle. She must have been in shock because she walked back and all I could hear was "Jillu" – my pet name in the family. The sight was horrific. Pieces of coal were still sticking to her, her complete frock was stuck to her, and she could hardly breathe.

In what must have been the fastest I've ever run in my whole life, I ran to the top of the road and bought a few tubes of burn oil, which was a yellow cream used for the purpose. Her skin peeled off when we took off her dress, and showed her raw little body. She was burnt almost to the bone. We applied the cream frantically, hoping that it would ease the pain for her. Susan wasn't responding. My mother screamed to my brother to get a rickshaw, which took forever, because one had to get to the top of the road to wait for one. We got in the rickshaw and raced to the nearest hospital.

She was bandaged from the shoulders to the hips for months, and the pain must have been unbearable. She was the sister whose life I saved when she was an infant, and to me she was the most precious thing in the world. She could have died, but heaven only knows how and why she didn't. She was already a very fragile child and had little or no flesh on her in any case; but thousands of tears, plenty of prayers, and a tremendous amount of love saw her through yet again.

The grocery shop that never asked
for payment

The tea shop that gave her family
free milk and helped save her
sister's life

CHAPTER TEN:
CHOCOLATE BOMBS

Throughout my entire life in India, from when I was a little girl to the time I left the country, we were always looked upon as being different – and, being British, not wanted there. This feeling manifested itself in various ways. People never ceased to make us feel humiliated, cheap, unwanted and abused, simply because of us being different in appearance from them. Although we were as poor as they were, the only difference was that we had different features. The colour of our skin, hair, and eyes made us into curiosities that were peculiarly attractive, yet despicable to them all at the same time.

India is a country where men outnumber women to a significant extent. In the place where we lived resided hundreds of men who followed us around, just to have us glance their way, failing which they called us names, or tried to touch us inappropriately. It gave them a sense of pleasure just to do so because we were fair and because we were different. We could not walk on the roads without every second man trying in some way to openly disrespect us.

When we were little, we were continuously called names like sada chua (white rat), sada murghi (white chicken), sada goo (white shit), sada tilchate (white cockroach), dasi mughi (foreign chicken), randi (prostitute) and many more. Vulgar gestures and sexual advances of every conceivable type were made with virtually every step you took. They resorted to the worst type of behaviour when they didn't get their own way, until we learnt to fight back. On the whole, it was not as bad as it was on the streets outside the school walls. We were sometimes ridiculed even more since we did not speak the language well at all, but we did what any human being would do – and that was to retaliate as best we could, using broken Hindi or Bengali, or whatever we could speak at the time.

We dressed in Western clothes, were independent, forward-thinking, and somewhat irrepressible and outspoken. Brought up like that at home, we never allowed ourselves to be subdued and controlled. Because of our western outlook and our aversion to dominate or be cruel to another human being, we were branded 'sluts' – why?

The reasons seemed to be the reverse of what humane individuals would otherwise expect. Our parents allowed us to mix with any person as long as they were decent, respectful, loving and kind. That, along with the belief they ingrained in us that no one was bad until proved otherwise, became clearly unacceptable in a society where competition is the name of the game and where no-one is an exception to the rule. When it came to class warfare and navigating levels in society, we didn't act in the socially acceptable manner, according to a land of people where men are put on a pedestal irrespective of their intelligence, behaviour, attitude or mentality.

Evidently, our freedom of thought, word and deed was what was totally unacceptable to them. I guess that anything that cannot be explained or understood is criticised, and criticism was an understatement compared to what we faced. Except for a few restrictions due to the fact that we lived in such a bad area, my father never controlled, dominated, hurt or beat my mother, or any of us. My father and mother did not know better than to live and let live, to not subdue, judge or try to control another human being.

When the Indian children finally started to have fun with us, he encouraged us to be normal and live normally, instructing us to ignore the differences in physical appearance between them and us. My parents allowed us to express ourselves and be our own persons, even if we were female, despite the fact that this was considered to be taboo to everyone around us.

For these reasons, my father did not like to bring us home for the holidays. He worried that someone might physically abuse us, kidnap us, or, worse still, slash our faces with razor blades, which is exactly what happened to my older sister. He feared, in the event of us defending ourselves from the verbal or physical abuse, or protesting, we might be harmed in ways that he would rather not think about.

As we grew up into little ladies, on the occasions when one of our girls began a relationship with an Indian boy, his parents vigorously disapproved because of what his and all the other people in his society felt about us. Therefore, we were accused, convicted and condemned without them even knowing the kind of people we were. If we were Indian-English girls, we were automatically branded almost untouchable, whether they knew us, had ever set eyes on us, or heard about us as we really were. The truth wasn't important. We were a social stigma and we had to live with it.

The only matter of importance was the fact that our culture and way of life was unacceptable to them. Full stop. Therefore, if we didn't subject ourselves to living their way or marrying their way, we were abused by one and all. This harsh treatment over the years hurt us terribly, and we were mentally traumatised by the continuous defilement.

A few years after we moved into the Kidderpore area a huge building was erected directly in front of our house, onto the already densely overbuilt space it occupied. It blocked out every bit of natural light that there ever was, forcing us to keep our lightbulb on day and night. If not, it would be pitch dark in our room. To be honest, since we hardly ever had electricity anyway, it was pitch black in there most of the time, except for one candle burning.

The darkness-inducing building became a sari centre called The Sari Godown, which printed designs on saris to be sold in the market. The godown (factory) sported some extremely long tables on which workmen would put down a single-colour sari. Then, after dipping wooden stamps of all sizes into colour or paint, they'd stamp the saris, which came out looking beautiful. The owner took a liking to us, and on occasion he allowed us to watch movies on a small television while lying on those tables. My father was okay with the arrangement, since he could just take a single step outside the house, open the door of the huge godown, and could look in to ensure that we were safe.

It was wonderful when the owner bought us cakes and chocolates, and even dinner. One day while my siblings and I were lying in a row on the table, watching a movie, the owner stood to the side and put his hands into my panties. Being so young, I wasn't sure if it was right or wrong. He was smiling at me and I wasn't being hurt, so I thought nothing of it. When I think of the incident today, I now know, of course, what was going on, and feel extremely upset about it.

He was an otherwise respectable man, someone who was well regarded in society for his business, his class, his name. He had a wonderful family, and everything else. He appeared to be very decent to my parents, someone who could have been trusted. Because I was aware that he could make life extremely difficult for us in that area, my parents never ever knew about the molestation.

Moreover, my silence meant something a little pleasant for me and the rest of my siblings for a change – treats like movies and ice cream, about which we could only ever dream. I decided never to say a word and didn't tell my parents anything. To me it was a small price to pay for their peace of mind, and to help prevent us from being violated or from something even more drastic happening to our family. Should the truth have come out, I could have caused more harm than good.

This, and other inappropriate behaviour, continued over a period of time and became more and more frequent. Eventually, it came to the point where I stopped going to the godown altogether. I never did tell my parents or anyone else anything, as he sometimes helped them with small loans, and he occasionally handed my little sister and brother a rupee or two as well. Being Indian, and having a lot of power in the area, he could have harmed us in many ways. For all of these reasons I kept things quiet, but I never forgot.

Since most of us were girls, my mother had to accompany us to the head of the road most of the time, approximately two miles away. She had to ensure that we were not being followed or harassed, and that we were safe. Whenever we walked alone, virtually every man tried to abuse us. They would shout out slurs or make the most awful signs and gestures, which were humiliating beyond imagination. In order to try to shield us from as much as she could, my mother made every effort to accompany us whenever possible.

During Holi, the festival of colour which is meant to observe the advent of spring, people celebrate by putting colour on each other. For us, and even to this day in India, as you might imagine, Holi was a festival which was abused by vandals and was by no means a celebration. Months before the festival they would fill water balloons with coloured water and fling them at us, balloons bursting on our chests, heads, backsides, and faces. They aimed at us from high-rise buildings or younger men and even little children ran straight towards us, flinging them at us, laughing, abusing and running away. We tried to chase them in an attempt to fight back, but never caught them amongst the millions.

The most careful aim was taken to ensure we were humiliated and hurt to the maximum. When the balloons hit us it made us dizzy, and sometimes even sent us to the ground. We cried our hearts out but had no option but to brave the onslaught by continuing on our errands, walking down the road to find transportation or to buy food or take care of daily needs. As the New Year ended, we used to fear the approach of this festival. Even though we clad ourselves properly, kept our heads down, walked in broad daylight, and tried to avoid dangerous lanes of potential ambush, nothing stopped this vandalism and open abuse. It was worse than a nightmare.

Everyone on a street of hundreds of people used to

either stare or laugh. Not only were we covered in colour and our clothes ruined, but also our breasts used to pain. We were most often shaken, upset and humiliated, and yet we had to keep going. Unable to always grin and bear it, sometimes we would fold up right there and start crying. With no one around except men, who enjoyed the game, we would sometimes try to find a good-hearted woman, who might run over to scold them or bring us something to wrap ourselves in.

Sometimes we took a rickshaw to avoid the men lurking and leering at us from both sides of the street. Nervous and panicky, we had to cover up, worried at the thought of the men waiting to abusively drench us. Unrelentingly, unashamedly, they would still run along the side of the rickshaw and pelt us straight on with the balloons, and then run off. You could not think of walking down the road during those times because you would end up with all your clothes wrecked, everything covered with colour, or you would end up hurt. What's worse, they would throw the balloons at you from such a distance that sometimes your skin would split with the force at which it came at you. If you happened to get it on the head you saw stars, and it took a while to regain your composure. Getting hit on the breasts or in inappropriate places was the most humiliating – not to mention the sheer trauma of having to go through this for months on end, with no other way out but to endure.

They wanted to humiliate us, but the main reason they would do it was to get our clothes wet and make it cling to our bodies, so that our breasts or the shape of our bodies would show. This to them was entertainment, but it was something they never dared to try with an Indian girl. Sometimes we had to walk home with our hands over our chests, shivering, crying, and literally torn in body, mind and soul.

One day, my mother's arm was broken when a truck driver opened his door without looking to see if anyone was approaching. She was taken to the free hospital for an X-Ray. The man taking the X- Ray asked my little sister to stand with him by the machine and press the round green button. She thought he was being nice to her, a little nine-year-old girl worried about her badly injured mother. But while she pressed the button, he had his arm blocking her exit and fondled her breasts. He then allowed her back to my mother's side. Upset as she was, close to tears, she said nothing, because my mum was in so much pain. The last thing she wanted to do was to cause her any more distress. So, like me, she just endured.

Around the same time, when she was about nine or ten, my sister was running around with friends in the area where we lived and was cornered by a man who must have been more than twenty years old. He grabbed her hand, but wasn't letting go. Her friends had run on ahead by then and she was faced with trying to get away from him. She begged him to let her go. After looking at her and every part of her body in the most repulsive manner, he said to her in crude Hindi that he was letting her go then, but he would get her some day when she grew up. She was shaken and ran home, but told nobody. Because we were outnumbered, anything was possible at the hands of such people – and we knew it.

When we were insulted or humiliated in front of my mother, she always became upset, and would say, "Let it go, they don't know any better. Does it hurt? Show me where. Just don't say anything. Just leave it. There's too many of them. We are out- numbered." She sometimes tried to fight, but the battle was one-sided and the numbers were clearly against us. We could have lost everything but, worse still, we could have been murdered, raped, humiliated and forgotten about forever. If we dared to threaten a man's reputation, being Indian-English girls, we knew in all likelihood we would have been blamed and abused for provoking the reaction we got.

My parents used to try their best not to bring us home from school at all. They would just leave us there for as long as possible. In the years Easter coincided with the Holi Festival, we would be forced to be home for the holiday. Being subjected to what they called a festival was, in our experience, nothing short of the worst type of racial abuse that existed – requiring the utmost in human endurance to survive the suffering it caused.

My father always used to counsel us, saying "We are among the Philistines, so that's how we must treat this. There's no point in trying to fight, because if I try to fight one, I'll have a hundred of them upon me within seconds. So I can't fight. We can't fight. I can't even think of starting a fight. They'll just murder us here, because we are seriously outnumbered."

Even today, when I think of those days, I recall times when Dad and Mum could not contain their hurt or sadness. On a few of those occasions it did get to the point of heated words, especially when the Indian men had done something particularly awful to us. I remember us pleading with them, "Dad, Mum! Just leave it. Please don't say anything. Let it go. Let's get home."

We were truly terrified of them harming our parents in

front of our eyes, after which they undoubtedly would abuse us as well. For this reason alone, most of the unfortunate deeds were never ever brought to the attention of my parents or ever talked about. Most often we had to suffer in silence, pretending that nothing had happened or that something else was bothering us instead. We would share it among ourselves just to ensure that we informed each other of which men were the worst, the ones to run from, or would go into a shell for days until the next incident occurred.

Another festival, a festival of lights called Diwali, really made the presence of these so-called human beings known to us in reprehensible fashion. Not satisfied with making our lives a misery year round, they would also take sick pleasure by throwing huge 'chocolate bombs' and dynamite sticks into the narrow lane directly in front of our house and into our veranda. 'Chocolate bombs' are shaped and packaged like round balls of chocolate, filled with gunpowder, small nails and other little metal items. Frightening us to a degree that is virtually impossible to describe, the detonation they made was unbelievably dramatic, especially within a confined space such as the narrow lane, which was less than three feet wide. We used to lock the one little wooden door that we had, but the sheer detonation of the bombs would drive anyone insane, let alone children.

Obviously, throwing bombs into that narrow a space, the noise, the effect, the terror it caused was inhuman. The reverberation would ring in our ears for hours afterwards. The whole room, the whole area, the whole passage would be polluted with smoke, giving off the suffocating smell of burning gunpowder. As evening approached, we sat in that little room with our hands over our ears, and just waited in dread for the bombs to land.

Another explosive was called the 'chilli bomb', an array of small red bombs tied together along a string. Most often hundreds of these bombs were tied together on a single long string (you could buy them in rolls of hundreds), set afire, and dropped in front of our house – or literally inside our one little veranda. The deafening noise would carry on non-stop for a good ten to twenty minutes, and it felt as though it would never end. No sooner it did, than they used to throw another sheet of them down. Huddled together, cowering inches away inside, all we could do was sit stricken, literally trembling in fear. They would sometimes send rockets from straight-necked bottles through our curtains, and even into our house if we hadn't closed our door in time. It was like being in a war zone and sometimes even worse, with the sound and the fear that we had to endure for days on end. Most of our neighbours looked out for it as an opportunity to get to us, knowing that we couldn't bear it and were unnerved by it.

They would start throwing them months before Diwali, and continued on through a month afterwards. That time of the year was worse than when they openly hurt us with water balloons. They would throw bombs at our feet while we walked on the roads, nearing us as we passed. They wouldn't even bat an eyelid about throwing it straight at us, either. I remember when bombs landed at our feet as we rode in rickshaws. If we were lucky we could kick them back out before they exploded. You dared not go out or step out of your room, because they would just throw one at you just to watch it burn you – to cause you to fall and hurt yourself, all for them to laugh at. It was the cheap thrills they got at our expense that was beyond human comprehension.

From early afternoon or evening we were restricted right through to the morning. Most often we could manage to get out as early as possible, though not without encountering one abuse or another. We hurried to gather in some food and supplies, and prepared for the worst. We were forced to stay indoors, having to pee in a mug and get rid of it later, too scared to even go outside to the toilet that was just a few steps away. Sometimes there was no electricity for nights on end and we would be burning hot with unbearable humidity levels, but we had to remain boxed in at all costs in order to stay safe.

Those were very, very hard times. The lewd bullies carried on for years on end. They didn't care if there was a dying child in the house, or a two-year-old who was traumatised by the bombing, or even my father, who was a heart patient. They had no feelings whatsoever. We really couldn't fight back. How could we? Due to our desperate circumstances and our crippling poverty we were prisoners in the country we lived in, and it was more than traumatic. After the festival, there were a number who were burnt, hurt and injured. I remember families trying to console one another and I grew to detest these festivals. Just the thought of it scares me to death.

It was positively the most horrid of experiences. We did our best to console ourselves, but at the same time we anguished over the newborn baby in the house and my little brother, who was only two or four or six at the time. Until this day, despite all the hardship and trauma we endured, I'm not sure how we persevered through the suffering. Yet we survived, emerging from it, and ultimately did very well for ourselves.

That was the Festival of Lights, the festival of Diwali. The result carried forward is that I used to get startled at the least of things, and became timid to the point of panic. I am still not able to stand loud concussions like from a vehicle backfiring, or people enjoying normal Christmas crackers. I was scared of most things and felt unstable for a while even if so much as a balloon popped near me, or someone burst a cracker at Christmas. It affected my other siblings in different ways as well.

Today, we joke about it in the family. Even my little niece has learnt how to frighten me just for kicks. To be honest, it's affected both my sister and me in ways that are somewhat inexplicable, resulting in very different behaviours. She has become a no-nonsense person and fears no-one and nothing. Being much fairer and blonder than me, she, in a way, faced more of the abuse. She learnt to fight back at the drop of a hat, with no questions asked, in order to protect herself. On many an occasion, even though younger than I, she stood up for me and fought many of my battles. For my part, I went into a shell, so to speak. I became extremely nervous, timid, and lost every ounce of confidence. Even though I was alive, I went into a permanent shell of fear.

I suppose the fact that I spent more time at home, and hence endured much more, made me the more timid one, the one who will be more likely to back down than put up a fight. All I want is a peaceful, quiet, non-confrontational existence. Because of this, I've sometimes allowed people to take utter advantage of me. I was scared of swimming, driving, and tended to fear anything that meant any harm. Constantly having to persevere in situations during my childhood, where I was unable to do anything to help myself, has probably influenced my tendency to be fearful. Loud noises, any hint of violence, or the potential dangers in crowds of people were the most prevalent triggers.

I remember an occasion when we couldn't pay our rent, which at the time cost only 100 rupees a month (one pound and thirty pence). Even that was too much for my father to afford. That day he had gone to work and my mother had brought me home from school. When we arrived, human excreta had been smeared all over our door and our lock. It was horrible having to clean the door and the lock before letting ourselves in. No matter how much we tried, we still smelt, and my mother made us bathe in Dettol antiseptic. My father had faced it before when he had just left the army. He told us of how men used to run down the streets covered in holi, which means all the colours, with buckets of human excreta in their hands. They would then smear it on all the doors and locks of all the Christian households in the area.

We grew very angry and cried our eyes out, but we knew deep down that we had to endure it all, because we were poor and did not belong there. We couldn't change the way we looked, and had no way of escaping. Once again, my mother gave us to the strength to carry on. No matter the suffering in the face of many such incidents throughout our childhood and adolescence, she showed us the way to maintain our composure and dignity, to withstand them all; always reminding us that gratitude should come above all else.

My father always regretfully grieved about how he should have left for the UK when he had the chance, and blamed himself many times for putting us through this. His health didn't permit him to do so, and finding the money was another story. My parents were destined to live and die in India, but, with the most fervent of hopes, they always wanted us to leave so that the abuse would stop and our lives would, someday, get better.

The passage in which the chocolate
bombs were thrown. Jill's family
lived in a tiny room on the left.

CHAPTER ELEVEN:
A PERFECT STORM OF ADVERSITY

As I wrote earlier, during one year of our traumatic stay in Kidderpore, my mother kept me home from school for about eight months. Circumstances being as dire as they were, she had to have me take care of the little ones, so that she could go out doing odd jobs to add to the small income my father was making.

After all those long months, I arrived back to school feeling like I didn't know what had hit me. Despite that, somehow I managed to pass muster very well. I passed in every subject. Mrs Hurtis, my teacher at the time, awarded me the progress prize and congratulated me in front of the whole school for beating the odds and managing to pass the class.

Those remarkable results at school gave Mum the impression that I could readily make up for missed studies, so she just kept keeping me home to look after the little ones. This set a routine into motion where we switched on and off over many years. I looked after the children, then went to school – back to the board; and then came home for months at a time; and went back to the board again.

I was growing up playing a grown-up for real, with all the stakes of being a real mother. However, still a child at heart as well as in body, I saw no reason to be hateful. Despite all the hardship, I still had fun and liked to be high-spirited and playful and with Vanessa by my side. It was hard not to remain happy, since she was a child that allowed no one and nothing to affect her. She loved every day and sometimes cried and sometimes hurt, which was natural. But on most occasions she was amazingly strong; my pillar of strength in thought, word and deed.

Over time we grew up and got to an age where we could have boyfriends. We did and, being young, were very happy. We started feeling as all youngsters do.

This, however, was not to be as we were social untouchables and were not 'worthy' of such happiness. Historically, our girls have been bitterly disappointed. Some had their men run off abroad without telling them. Others were led to believe that they would be married to the man they loved, only to later learn that his wedding had been arranged elsewhere or that he had married without their knowledge.

A number of people whom I knew about have allegedly been raped just because they refused sexual advances, or refused to be friends with men they didn't want to be with.

Most of them have gotten no justice at all. Some of them have even been gang-raped and are still living with the trauma, the physical and emotional scars, and so much more that they don't even talk about it today. They live locked up in silence with the shame of more and more people getting to know what happened to them, rather than getting help for what is so radically restricting their lives.

I also have friends who allowed themselves to be duped by their trust in men – men who talked the girls into giving them their money, then bolted and ran off abroad. This scheme of profuse lying and deceit insidiously came about because, ultimately, they would never have been allowed to marry girls from our community.

There have been other cases where Indian men have fallen in love with an Indian-English girl, chosen to live with her, given her children, and then grown tired of the whole charade. Introducing an Indian-English girl into society was out of the question, for fear of ruining the 'respectable' reputation of the family. Our girls have been beaten until they were too frightened to challenge the man, and have even committed suicide since they were not accepted, through no fault of their own. Time to move on. They'd had their fun.

At the age of sixteen, I myself went out with a boy

whom my parents grew to like very much. He did like me, yet kept hesitating to tell his family about me. After a few months, I was told that his family would never agree to him seeing me, let alone marrying me. I was just an Indian-English girl, an untouchable, and not fit to be with him. I was shocked, and couldn't understand why I was being judged in this manner when I was just a simple school-going girl, but he explained that this was how his parents felt. It was not something that was even allowed to be talked about in his family. He explained that it wasn't him who felt the same way, but that he was helpless, and had no option in the matter.

It's amazing to realise that, without bothering to get to know a person, how easy it is for some people to pass judgement. Irrespective of the reputation one has or the soul one has, they make up their minds to condemn you for no fault of your own. You are believed to be an untouchable, and that is how you will be looked upon forever. Is that truly fair? In my life and that of the people around me, it was. My life in no way, shape or form has been that of a prostitute, yet my boyfriend was scared to death just to be seen with me in public, in case he happened to meet a family member or a friend who would inform his family that he was out with a girl like me. This would mean dire consequences for him, and the fact that no decent Indian family would allow their daughter to marry him, if he was ever seen with a girl like me.

Even though he would always say that "You have a heart of gold and are one good girl", he could not overcome the fright that his family had instilled in him. He could never come to terms with facing up to them and telling them about me. To this day, I always get emotional when I listen to Dolly Parton's song Chicken Every Sunday, because it always makes me think of my mother, who reminded me of this song when people looked down upon us (especially when it was a boyfriend). The only difference was that Dolly's song relates to her being poor, but we were both poor and different – and for that we paid a very heavy price.

On the other hand, there were also some – a handful – who were very kind to us as well, and never judged us. They loved and respected us for who we were. These were 'good souls', as my mother would call them. Despite being the poorest of the poor, illiterate, and totally insignificant, they nevertheless were people who at times virtually saved our lives.

Simple people like a meat man most often gave my mother either credit or packed up meat regularly, even giving extra at times, knowing that we were quite a few kids, and very poor. There were grocer's men who gave us vegetables without taking money even though they were extremely poor themselves, but again only gave it because they knew we hadn't eaten. There was a corner shop man who gave us credit on a regular basis, but never asked to be paid. He always waited until the rare times my parents would try to pay him.

For Christmas we had to wear school shoes until we were fourteen years of age. Our sponsors used to send the school money for us at Christmas, and we were allowed one outfit and one pair of shoes each only. My mother always made us buy school shoes, since she didn't have the money to buy us the school shoes later if we spent the money on a fashionable pair instead. We were teenagers by then and felt rather stupid dressed in school shoes, while all the other girls were well-dressed in fancy shoes and other fineries. We had to watch our friends bring so many little things to school that girls love, things we only dreamt about, whereas we would return to school with not even the basics.

Never ever had we stolen anything from anyone. If we didn't have something, we did without. My father always saw to that, saying things like, "If I left a penny on a table and came back after ten years, I expect to find the penny right where I had left it." Plainly and simply, this is what he called honesty. We respected our parents and loved them for everything they did for us. It always hurt to think that, through no fault of their own, our parents were forced to stay in India, where their sad fate in life was sealed, and where we too paid a very heavy price.

Yes, we were poor. Yes, we were malnourished. We might not have been able to pay our rent and we didn't have much food or anything that other kids our age had. We were very far from being well-off and actually lived in partial starvation, and in housing equivalent to slums or worse. We hardly had any clothes, and sometimes just longed for a toy to play with, or a good meal. We were all of this. But there was something we were not. We were positively not the sluts or prostitutes we were being branded as.

The biggest price we have paid until now, through it all, was being branded sluts by the very society we lived in – whether or not they knew us, whether or not they knew the hardship of the life we had led, and irrespective of how hard we tried to better our lives through honesty, hard work, and perseverance. Irrespective of any understanding of us as human beings, who loved them very much and just wanted to be loved in return. To them we were still sluts, or 'white trash'.

People from India (mainly South India) ,who have no British ancestry at all, write articles and stories about our community that are sometimes very hurtful. They set themselves up as being authorities on the subject and want to show the world how much they really know about us. In truth, they know very little or nothing at all; they only have their projections of racial prejudice to fling at us. A very unfair and hypocritical society indeed.

Taking my case in question: if one were to speak to my family, my friends, my employers, and many others, they will confirm how far away I am from this notion and this very hurtful word 'slut'. I'm mentioning this in my book only because there are still many girls out there who are still living the same kind of existence and enduring the humiliation, whether or not they deserve it.

Indian-English people on the whole are people with some of the biggest hearts. The humility, humbleness, kindness, humanity, love and care that our people have and demonstrate are rare. Yes, we may have our faults too...but doesn't everybody? I am very proud to be Indian-English, proud of my ancestry, and proud of the work my community have done and continue to do in India without expecting anything in return. We are a race that will help anyone without even knowing them, and who love and help unconditionally.

Case histories such as mine underscore the reasons why enduring endless obstacles and overcoming them makes one stronger and more resilient. Fighting uphill battles may have kept some of the Indian-English from being the most highly educated of people, and we may not have ranked at the top. Nevertheless, there are quite a few Indian-English doctors, bankers, teachers, artists and professionals with significant accomplishments.

Many an expatriate needs to look no further when they return to India to open a new business and need the support of an intelligent, bright, proactive and well-mannered Indian-English girl. On many occasions, I have been requested by others to recommend girls from our community for top Executive Assistant roles. Some of these roles pay more than that of many highly paid Executives, and for a reason. What's disturbingly sad about this kind of thing is that, when a native girl earns it, it's looked upon as being highly respectable and prestigious. But the minute an Indian-English girl earns it, it's put down to the fact that we could only have earned so much because we are indecent, have used our looks or our bodies to have got the job. In truth, virtually every top support role was held by an Indian-English girl. We are headhunted and competitively sought after for the same kinds of positions. When I lived and worked in India, a review was done on the top salaries earned by Executive Assistants in the country, and I came out at the top of the list. I can assure you, however – and, as you've seen throughout the book so far – that it wasn't because of illicit affairs that I had with any senior executives!

Like any other minority community, we too have good and bad. To be honest, the majority of us have had it harder in life than most, and yet we not only have persevered, endured and survived, but have also given back to the very communities who, through no fault of our own, have abused us for most of our lives. We do not paint everyone with the same brush, nor do we judge people for what their fathers have done, or what their background or parentage or beliefs have led them to do.

I know very many senior executives for whom I have worked, both in India and in London, who would readily do anything for me – and why? I can absolutely assure you that it's not because I'm a 'slut', but rather because I've earned it, worked for it, and proved myself in order to receive the recognition and testimonials that verify my character and dedication to work. For all of this, I am very proud.

Having done everything the honest way, I used every little opportunity I found in my path to better myself. On most occasions, it was to look after many Indian children, the aged, and others who need help. In talking to many Indians, they say they wouldn't and couldn't have done what I have. Yet, to this day, the girls from my community and myself are still looked at and called sluts by many an Indian – they believe it's their birthright to call us that. It's a racist generalisation that has been handed down for generations.

Being a Christian, I have been brought up not to judge another person; but should people feel the need to do so, then they should stop to consider who and what others really are before branding them. I have written and dedicated my life and this book on behalf of people all over the world who face various types of abuse. Whom they are branded to be is never reality-based, nor close to indicative of who they really are as people, our fellow human beings. Like all of us, they are in search of freedom and happiness. It only pains the heart and bruises the soul to recognise that, while many recover from the atrocious societal wounds hurled at them, still many, many others don't. With the changing times, it would be wholly and reverently worthwhile to look at the colour of one's soul; not the colour of one's skin.

Jillian and Vanessa

CHAPTER TWELVE:
HOMAGE TO A NOBLE FIGHTER

Emaciated, exhausted and mentally shattered, my mother might have lost touch a little. Her concentration on the family sometimes lagged, because she was so sick from cancer and was totally drained. She had endured too much for too long. It was like she just couldn't go on any longer. She had lost her strength, her health, and the will to live.

She kept going only because she still had two little ones to care for. Even though she knew that the odds were against her, she fought desperately every day in order to do all she could to stay alive and to be there for them. Unfortunately, life does not give you extra points for the suffering you endure. Instead, the harsh reality is that, even after a lifetime of virtually intolerable and unbearable circumstances, comes the part where you are forced to pay the price of neglect, be it in any form, whether it's intentional or unintentional. In her case, it was time for her to pay with her life for a lifetime of constant sorrow, struggle, unwavering sacrifice and true neglect of herself.

Life brings no mercy to bear on one's past, good-natured intentions, love shown to others, or on what one endures. The body is a machine that breaks down when not cared for, and the breakdown comes in the form of terminal illness and human suffering. The worst is never over; it's always yet to come. The choice is always yours, and her choice was to sacrifice herself in order to save the lives of her family. This was apparent, and no amount of sadness, pain or questions as to why this had to happen to her was going to reverse the truth – the truth that she had cancer, the truth that this meant even more suffering, and the truth that she was going to die.

In school for stretches of time, then at home again taking care of the young ones and my mother and then going on into my youth, caring for them solely, I became in so many words the pillar of the family. Once I finished school, my father decided that I should be moved out of the area to avoid dire circumstances. My father took me by train to my elder sister's house while my younger sister Vanessa left to study to be a teacher in the city of Pune (formerly Poona) and the two little ones were by then in boarding school. When I reached Delhi, my elder sister did all she could for me, but was just about getting on her feet herself, and therefore could not look after me or pay for my further education. It came to the point where it felt best that I should leave her domain.

A couple that were friends but basically strangers to me took me in and looked after me. Graciously, when I started to study, they paid for my whole course and for a great portion of my subsistence, looking after me like one of their own. I will remain forever grateful to them and have tried in every way to return the debt.

I later moved in with my eldest sister Barbara, who had moved from Bombay to Delhi, and it was there that I found my first job. I remember her coming with me for my first interview and giving me all the support and courage I needed to get through that interview. It meant taking a bus ride quite a way from where she lived, and it is a daily journey I made that will live with me forever.

There were two sets of doors on the bus. People hung out of it every which way, as there must have been at least one hundred crammed into it. Invariably, I would get on at the front exit and try to sit in the first seat, just so that I could get off easily without having to push my way through to the exit and be physically abused on the way. Most days there was one particular lady who used to sit at the window seat of the bus. I would do my utmost to sit near her or beside her – firstly, because she was female and it felt so much better not to have to encounter physical advances by men, and secondly, being closest to the exit, it was easier to get off.

The lady got off a few stops before me and I always tried to move into her seat, away from the main aisle, because there were men who would hang or rub their testicles on my shoulder everyday. I would hunch down, sink lower and lower to avoid this pathetic degradation, yet they would seem to get wetter and wetter. I used to be in tears sitting there, just wanting my stop to arrive.

I remember a friend (an Indian girl) who gave me a safety pin, urging me to use it, but I never had the guts to do so. I used to hold my bag as close as possible to my chest so that they could touch me anywhere else. In any event, I couldn't even so much as look up without a man being right, there making inappropriate gestures and advances at me. Apart from these untoward advances happening, the minute the lady got up to get off the bus some of the men competed to scoot in across my lap in order to sit near me. There were those who used to try to beat the others to it by coming through the windows, feet first, in order to sit near me, resulting in their shoes touching me, rubbing mud and dirt all over my clothes. All of this was done just so that they could get near to me and be able to touch me or rub against me at some point during the journey. I hated going to work – and yet, worse was still to come.

I worked for an Export Company whose business was to send professional manpower to the Middle East. At first I was glad to have joined, because all I wanted was to try to earn in order to help my family. Being a family business, however, the son and the nephew took total advantage of their positions and used to harass me to go out with them. When I refused, I was made to work late. This meant they would be forced to drop me home by car. There was no other possibility by which I could even get to the nearest bus stop, approximately three miles away, without being abused en route.

Meanwhile, that area was under development with a lot of building and construction work underway, which meant that the area was full of men. Leaving work at that time of night, it was pitch dark outside with no lights at all. There were no women on the street – only loads of sand, cement, stones and building materials, and hundreds of men standing or sitting on the roadside.

I would have rather chosen to die there at work than venture to the bus stop on my own, and therefore I would have to accept their offers either to the bus stop or home. Most often the drops were unbearable, and meant I'd have to play the game in order to avoid unwanted sexual

147

behaviour.

In desperation, I agreed to be friendly with one guy who agreed to pick me up after work and drop me home. This was a relief because it kept the other guys at bay and was getting me home safely, for which I was very grateful. The rides continued until I soon discovered that he had failed to mention that he was married with five kids, with a wife who never left the house. Beginning to learn the hard way, I was hurt less by the fact that he was married than by the fact that I once more had to face getting home after work on my own.

What hurt the worst, though, was the fact that he said that his friends had told him that this was his opportunity to have sex with a foreign girl. Thankfully, he never got that far. I may have been just eighteen, felt alone and very confused with the world, very worried about my job (since he was a relative of the boss), and even more concerned than before about how to get home at night – but I emerged with my dignity intact. The downside was that I had to start taking rides home again from the owner of the company for a while, until, in desperation, I had no other alternative but to leave and find another job. There were no severance payments made, so it became a matter of working for one company for a month and the next for another, while I searched for something permanent.

By then my mother's condition had deteriorated to where she was hardly managing from day-to-day, prompting my father to write to me, telling me: "If you people, (meaning 'me and my sisters') want to see your mother alive in the next few months, you need to take her to Delhi for treatment, or you will lose her."

My mother would never say it, but – if I picture her now, and if I think back – her eyes were speaking for what her broken heart wasn't saying. Reduced to skin and bones at that time, she came to Delhi for treatment, because it was impossible in Calcutta to get anything done. Besides, there was no one else to take care of her, since my father simply had to keep his job in order to pay the bills, and support the little ones in school at the time.

The rest of the family now had their own families to take care of, their own problems, their own children and so on. The truth was that they had their own lives and were struggling to make ends meet themselves, and they couldn't take on anyone else on a permanent basis. Life was too hard already, and accepting responsibility for someone who was not just terminally ill but who also had two little ones to care for was asking too much. They helped every now and then but, unfortunately, could not take care of her for any length of time. I'm sure that she knew that their thoughts were always with her and that sometimes, as hard as things may seem on the surface, people do the best they can with the resources they have. It takes a special kind of person to believe that, and my mother was just that type. She not only understood and believed, but loved each of them dearly until the day her eyes closed.

In those days, I had no idea who I really was. I had no idea where I was going, or what life had in store for me. All I knew then, as I did always know, was that here before me stood my mother. She brought me up, and did the best she could. The two little ones were my flesh and blood, and far too little to be dealing with the death of their mother. I refused to see them put through the anguish of not being wanted, not being loved, and not having anyone to turn to. I may not have been the eldest but, since I was the only one who was not married at the time, it was understood that I had to take them over. There was not even a moment's hesitation or deliberation in making the decision. I wanted their happiness before mine. I wanted my mother and them to know that they had someone who cared – maybe not a person who had much to give, but just someone who promised I'll be there for you.

This meant, once again, that I had to carry the whole load. I brought my mother to Delhi where I took her to a free hospital, which was chaotic, filthy and horrible – but without any money, there were no alternatives. On any given day, there were hundreds of poor people who lined up just for a blood test or a scan. There were hundreds who streamed in and out of the hospital, most of them coming in from slums or nearby villages, destitute people who didn't even know where to go. It was just a sea of swarming people trying to get someone to help, and some kind of medical assistance.

Once you started the process of registering a patient, you were lucky if you got it done in the next three to five days. Each time, the patient needed to be present, so that the person doing the registration could see the patient. It meant people in long unruly queues with ailing patients, many of them too sick to even know where they were. Most were in colossal amounts of pain, screaming and moaning. You had to be patient, be grateful, and see it through.

Life was worse than impossible to handle. Being different from all the others added more pressure to make it almost unbearable. We were looked upon by the poor in a way that snarled: How come people like you are queuing among us? How come you all are so poor? Of course, it was a golden opportunity for men, who thought that we were now their equals.

In this miserable fashion, spending the day in such chaos meant accepting anything and everything that came at you. I would sometimes not even be able to get to work, but my boss (a German gentleman) was possibly the most understanding human being alive. He never got upset or warned me. I couldn't help but think that, even through the most difficult of times, there is always an angel in disguise on the sidelines helping you to get through life.

I managed to admit her to hospital and, after weeks of endless struggle and sheer resilience, arranged for an operation, followed by radiotherapy. The whole struggle was equivalent to getting to the moon and back. She was in hospital for seven months. Every morning I went to see her, clean her, feed her, and sit with her, and then went to work. In the evening, I returned to the hospital to be with her.

After a month, I started to live there most of the time. My boyfriend, who was an Indian-English boy, gave me all the support he could. He was an amazing person with a heart of gold, gifted with an inner strength and humility that most people don't possess today. With no questions asked, no expectations in return, and never caring about his own life, he more than willingly took care of my little brother who was a handful and by no means easy to control. I had to bring him to Delhi, since my father was by then too old to take care of him. My boyfriend took care of everything at home while I was at the hospital.

To ensure that my journey was a little easier, he tried to come with me on most occasions. He helped with my mother. He helped me bathe her, dress her, feed her, and tried in every way possible to make life as easy as he could for her. He was not just another person sent in disguise to help, but an individual for whom I shall be forever grateful, without whose help I might never have made it through those times of unimaginable suffering.

An established routine developed for me – months and months of living in a hospital, just going home long enough to collect a change of clothes, then back to living in at the hospital, going back and forth from there to work. I hardly ever went home. There were times when we had to sit on the floorboards of the bus just because there were no seats left. I was dropping with exhaustion, and couldn't cope any longer. I was at breaking point but all I could think of was one thing – I wanted my mother to survive.

With people sitting all over the corridors, in the

passages, down the aisles and in the main receptions throughout the day or night, the hospital was more than a depressing place to lodge. To get through the crowds was another story. Sick people were all over the place, waiting for the mornings in order to queue up again. Illness, poverty and squalor are mild compared to the suffering that was being endured within the grounds of that most inhospitable environment.

I'm sure every other free hospital is like it or worse, given the millions who live below the poverty line in that country. Everything reeked of either vomit, urine or phenyl (disinfectant) that was so powerful you could smell it even before entering the hospital grounds. Tears just came automatically to you when you heard people cry out in pain, when you saw them sitting hunched on the floor, holding their stomachs, their backs, their heads.

People were just left lying on stretchers everywhere. Staff were not able to cope with the volume of sick people. There were women screaming and crying, bashing their heads against the walls due to loved ones just having passed away; children crying and going to the toilet behind pillars or on paper, everywhere; people trying to get through in a great hurry; aged people who could stand no longer; food and linen scattered everywhere. In the midst of it all, there I was, hoping against hope to save the life of my mother, against all odds.

To make a bad situation worse, outside the hospital there were students setting themselves on fire, in protest against the government who were giving reservations to schedule castes and schedule tribes instead of to those students who were being college-educated. Times arose when I couldn't even get near the hospital. There were bombs, riot police, soda water bottles being thrown, tear gas being used by the police, and students setting themselves on fire. There were lengthy protests, processions that lasted for miles on end, police that were outnumbered a thousand to one, and violence that was of the worst kind. Despite it all, I somehow got through every day, just to see my mother and take her a juice or something to eat. She was too sick to even know what ordeals I had to navigate in order to get to her.

The scene was one of the most depressing ones I have ever had to visit; but human endurance is such that when a loved one's life depends on it, all else is forgotten. I didn't even think of myself, or what might happen if a bomb went off or if I got caught in a riot or the possibility of being trampled to death. My focus was on getting to my mother's bedside, and I did.

We were lucky, in a small way, because of a medical student named Dr Sandeep Uppal. He was training to be a doctor at the hospital at the time, an Indian boy that used to take drum lessons from my brother-in-law. He was another devoted individual who had clearly pledged his life to help others. Consciously choosing to be there working with some of the worst cases on earth was in itself a laudable virtue. He did whatever he could to make life easier for us at that hospital. Were it not have been for him, we might never have had the ability or the strength to carry on as much as we did. It was an impossible task.

Having this one connection, knowing someone who worked there, was a lifeline. Things could have been a lot worse without him, beyond which he had a heart of gold and loved my mother like his own. He was just a student himself and had to make a lot of personal sacrifices in order to make time to help her, but moving forward without him was on most occasions asking the impossible. Rarely do you find a doctor with so much compassion, or encounter a younger boy with so much love and care for people in need. I marvelled as I watched him frequently stop and talk to people, lend them a hand, show them the way, give them advice, and do just about anything throughout the day, while the other doctors didn't even stop to answer. Caste, creed, religion, colour, race aside; this person was different.

We existed in that putrid atmosphere, facing death and the reality of life every day, where we were exposed to the true side of a human being under immense pressure. Very rarely do you ever find someone so inspiring in your midst. He was the kind of person often found shining in the worst of circumstances, a gifted leader. Not just talented or intelligent or bearing a title, but here was someone notably different. My family and I owe this doctor much gratitude – not just for helping my mother, but also for being there when no-one else was. It is said that people come into your life for a reason. I believe this is true, and see this instance as nothing short of a miracle.

Although I was there for her every possible moment, the suffering never seemed to abate for my mother. She was released and came home for a few days but then, worrying about my father and my youngest sister, went back to Calcutta. In no condition to travel and in need of intensive care and attention herself, her love for them could not keep her away. We let her go, but it was then that her condition worsened. My little sister was brought home from school to administer to her. She used to dip a rag in warm water and then rub it on her back to try and ease her pain. The cancer was malignant, yet my mother just carried on from day to day as best she could.

My mother's condition worsened. Receiving her back to Delhi, I took her to another free hospital way across the city, which meant even more hardship in order to get her any kind of treatment. She was admitted to hospital once again and given radiation therapy, growing weaker and weaker on a daily basis.

I took all my emoluments, benefits and salary a year in advance from the company I worked for, just to be able to buy her medicines, some food and nourishment everyday. I did everything I could to save her life. Unfortunately, a brain scan proved that the cancer had returned and spread. It had grown up her spine and all over her skull. The doctor told me that it was only a matter of days before the cancer would touch her brain, and she would die.

While on her last trip to Calcutta, she had somehow fractured her shoulder bone. It is known that tumours often grow to where they will break bones. She couldn't understand why they were not setting her hand in plaster, and asked the doctors everyday to re-set her arm. They kept telling her they would schedule a date to do that. I visited her as usual one evening after work, and the doctor took me a few yards away from her bed. Privately, he told me that she had approximately fourteen days or so to live, and that I should take her home.

I remember that moment, remaining at the doorway of the ward, thinking about what I had just been told. She was looking at me with eyes that knifed right through me. The doctor asked me if I was okay and I said yes, thanked him for everything. The only thought that came to me was: what else could I do to reverse this diagnosis? Why had everything I had done not worked? I think I had lost my ability to concentrate, or I may have lost my mind for a few seconds.

I walked toward her in a daze, wanting dejectedly to give up, to hold her, and to cry my heart out, when she brought me to my senses by asking "What did the doctor say?" Composing myself with a deep breath, I had to look straight at her, and answered, "I had asked if I could take you home for a few days, since you've been here a long time. And he was advising me of what to do if I did take you home tomorrow."

She was excited, and said, "So, come on then – let's go." I replied, "No, Mum. We have to wait until tomorrow since we have to get all the paperwork signed, and no staff are around right now." She bought the story.

I sat with her, and fed her, and talked to her. I rubbed

her back, combed her hair, and kissed her good night. I wanted to stay with her forever but I also wanted to leave, to bolt out of there and just cry my heart out. On the other hand, I couldn't bear the thought of leaving her side for a single moment. I was a robot just steeling myself, barely able to hold back the flood of tears and the breakdown that inevitably would follow the slightest letting down of my resolve. The minute I walked out of the ward, I felt a loss and grief that I will never be able to describe. I had been through a lot with, and for, this woman who was my mother. After all that she had done for us, been through, and the fight that I had put up for her, the thought of losing her was unbearable.

Stopping every few steps – feeling absolutely alone, weak and incapable of being able to do anything to change the words of the doctor – I cried all the way home, and couldn't care who was looking at me or not. I could not stop crying. I was in a state of fear, shock, terror, depression, and God knows what else. I remember thinking: did I hear right, or was it just the stress and the tiredness that was catching up with me? I had a roiling mixture of feelings and felt sick to my stomach. I thought that I had saved her, having been told only a few years ago that her cancer was in remission. I remember sitting on the bus, a thousand emotions all running through me at the same time, in turmoil to think that she had had such a sad life. She had fought right through every wretched obstacle wrenched into her path, and never really did have anything to be happy about. And I? All I wanted was to be given the opportunity to care for her and to take care of her for a short while longer. I just didn't want my mother to die!

Trying to control myself but not being able to do so, I do not know how I got home or how the rest of the night went by. I do recall that the following day my younger brother went to see her and she came home with him. Still fighting to save her, I resumed nursing her and refused to accept what the doctor had said. I thought that it wasn't right and that we could nurse her back to health. I was in a state of denial. I still thought that a miracle could save her, too.

She kept asking as to why they were not setting her arm and asked if it was because she was going to die. I told her no, that they were worried that the anaesthetic might react with the strong medicines she was currently on; and therefore they were waiting for her condition to improve a bit, which is when they would stop the medicine and set her arm.

She was pleased with that, but the pain that she was

going through with the cancer was, by comparison, dwarfing the pain in her arm. I did ask the doctor if her arm hurt and they said she didn't even feel it due to the amount of morphine she was on. I was relieved, but her condition worsened by the day. I had to sponge her, feed her (just liquids), and stay up with her virtually all night.

Within a week, she had slipped into a coma. The hardest thing I have ever had to do was to borrow money, order her coffin, and make funeral arrangements, well before she had died. I had even spoken to the caretaker of the cemetery where I had the plot dug up and made ready. We were told that in her condition we should not attempt to keep the body, but there was a part of me that still felt that she would wake up and feel better. I hated myself for preparing to bury her when she was still alive. I loved her more than ever, but was living every day in total turmoil just trying to do what I could and should do; all the while blaming myself at the same time.

By then, I was almost poverty-stricken myself and wasn't receiving any salary at all. Scratching out an existence, I was surviving on loans, and small amounts that my office gave me in order to help me buy her medicines and necessities. I had one small room, one bed and one steel closet and nothing more. Every moment and every penny earned went on trying to save my mother's life and on taking care of my little brother.

The only thing she asked, before she slipped into the coma, was to look after my younger two siblings for her. I promised, and have kept my promise ever since.

One morning in September, I woke at around five-fifty am to check on her, and she was still breathing. I moved her hair, patted her, and lay down again on the floor at her bedside. When I found myself sitting at her bedside once again it was six am, and she had just gone.

I sat with her for a long time, telling her "I know that you are still here, and you know how much I love you. Please stay with me and help me to look after the little ones. I promise never to leave them." And I remember feeling a silence that I have never felt before. I kissed her and closed her eyes fully. I kept looking at her with mixed emotions, thinking of what a strong woman I had as a mother and how honoured I was to have been given the opportunity to spend these precious moments with her.

We had a one room place, and usually by that time you could hear a hundred people filling water, walking about, vegetable men shouting out, and so on. But there was pin drop silence for a long period of time, before I woke my boyfriend and told him that I thought she had just gone.

He checked, and said it was true.

I remember going to my elder sister's house to inform her, and her husband said "Now that you've given us the news, you can fuck off!" I couldn't believe that a person could be so inhuman and so hurtful at a time like that but I guess it takes many types to make a world. Even though I was numb while I walked down their steps, it never hurt as badly as the thought of my mother lying in my house with no life at all. I understand today that people are not their behaviours, that he is truly a lovely person and should not be judged by his behaviour alone – no-one should be. It's for this reason alone that I decided to include this point in the book, to show people that people don't always mean what they say (good or bad) and it's this thought process that allows you to let go and to forgive. As is quoted in the Emerald Tablet, 'As within, so without' – in other words, if negative thoughts and emotions are suppressed, the outcome can never be positive.

I informed my other sister Barbara, who came right away to be with me, and we buried her the same day. When I informed my father, he was absolutely quiet on the phone. Because of health and financial reasons, he couldn't make it to her funeral. I knew it hurt him more than ever; but the less he heard of how much she suffered, the better he could manage the personal pain he felt.

In honour to my mother and respecting her wishes, also knowing that my father was far too old to take care of my little sister in school, I went to Calcutta soon after my mother's death and brought my little sister back to Delhi to live with me, where I put her in school. My father stayed in the same little room back in Calcutta for a while until he, too, finally came to stay with me in Delhi.

For a good six months after that day, I went to the cemetery every day after work and sat by my mum's grave to cry. All I could think about is how hard I fought to save her, how I just wanted to pull her out of there – and how I was ever going to cope on my own with two children and no money, since I had to work for the rest of the year without any salary at all. I knew that the sadness, the poverty, and the hardship had to change. I had made up my mind that this had to end...at least for the little ones, if not for me. We had endured an unbearable amount of hardship, and things just had to change. Someone had to make the change, and I was going to be that person.

CHAPTER THIRTEEN:
GOING AWAY

After my mother passed away, I was numb and in a state of shock for months later. I was just out of my teenage years, in a first job, grieving for a mother who had been the central emotional pillar for our family. Suddenly I found myself fully responsible for two very young siblings and my aged father, acting as the sole breadwinner for my family.

I remember, shortly after, talking to my father. He said to me that I'd had it hard from a young age, and reminded me of the quotation that he sent me in a letter:

There is a compensation for every cross you bear

A secret consolation is hidden somewhere there

If only you can find it; If only you can wait

An angel comes to comfort the lost and desolate.

These words proved prophetic. A short while later, I received a call from a job agency asking if I would be interested in applying for a better role that paid more money, as Executive Assistant to the CEO of American Express.

I was sure that there were many girls better-qualified

than me, but for some reason thought I would give it a go. I started the interviewing process with more than sixty-odd other girls. As luck would have it, I got through several rounds of tests and evaluations. At the final interview with the country head I somehow struck a chord, and was offered the job. He later told me it was the strong sense of sincerity and honesty that came shining through that made him offer me the role. I was elated at the opportunity, as it meant I could fulfil my responsibilities better and hopefully heralded the fact that, at long last life, was starting to get better.

That proved to be a sort of turning point for me in career terms. My boyfriend, the two little ones, and I moved to better accommodations. We led better lives, and were beginning to be a little happier. We tried to put most of the sadness behind us. Two years later, my boss moved back to the US but I picked up a similar role at the Bank of America.

I joined Bank of America in 1995 and remember being told that rumour had it I was hired because I was a foreigner and looked different. This was not true, because I had not only gone through a very rigorous interview process, but had also refused the job when I discovered that the job was currently being held by my father's best friend's sister. She was somebody I had seen intermittently while growing up – I thought of her as Aunt June, and respected her tremendously.

She was very good to me and, on learning that I had turned down the role, she called me and explained that she was moving on into a customer service role that she had always wanted, and would be very happy for me to have the role. The CEO was struck by my regard for my predecessor, and actually significantly increased the offer to make sure I joined. Having being reassured by her, I accepted and took the position, because I needed the money in order to change our lives.

It was good and bad, actually, because I did really well at work, and soon I was also appointed President of Bank of America's charity network in India, in charge of four metropolitan cities. My role was extremely demanding, and I was often working fourteen or fifteen-hour days – sometimes seven days a week. The country head was a very driven professional who had taken on the India role as a challenge, and worked extremely hard to meet his objectives.

As a result, he wanted to work all possible hours and days, and expected everyone in his team, especially me, to keep up with him. I was determined to succeed and was conscious of the responsibilities and people depending on me, and did what it took to make sure I was delivering despite the odds. I sometimes collapsed under the pressure, frequently getting home at two in the morning, and taking very few days off – even public holidays – because I was called into work.

I was managing two roles: Executive Assistant to the CEO and President of the Bank of America Charity and Diversity Network. Working with several fellow employees and a group of charities, I spearheaded drives to introduce many schemes designed to help the poor, the aged, the deaf and dumb, the blind, and many more disadvantaged people. Apart from that, I worked on an employee diversity network programme, which involved me taking community volunteers out on weekends to various hospitals, institutes, aged homes, charity centres, slums, and other areas of abject poverty and deprivation. I arranged several events to boost employee morale, diversity and unity within the bank and the community.

Despite doing two jobs and spending most waking hours at the office, I was at my best when I was out with the poor, the needy, the people who were on their deathbeds, and people who had no one to care for or to love them. I found that was the time when I felt totally

169

happy and content. The stress and tension of long days at work seemed to evaporate and I was ready for anything, because I felt great that I was making a difference, in whatever small way, to people's lives. I remembered how grateful I had been for the small gestures of kindness I had experienced growing up, and how much they had meant to me in those days.

The good work the bank had started doing with all the charities put Bank of America India on the global corporate map from a charity and diversity perspective. I emerged as the leader responsible for driving this work that had made employees feel they were giving something back to society, as well as raising the bank's profile in the country.

In recognition of the work done, the bank sent me to the worldwide headquarters in California to receive the Bank of America Individual Achievement Award. I had been selected out of all network contributors across a group of thirty different countries. I received the Service Excellence Award for dedication to the company and contribution to staff, as well as the Global Chapter of the Year Award for the publicity that the bank received due to the extensive charity schemes undertaken by the bank in India.

Those years were just amazing. I travelled a lot and delivered on every front, for which they actually recognised and awarded me many times over. I was very pleased and grateful and was able to send my siblings to a good school, and even to provide them with extra tuition in order to help them do well.

I did all of this while working daily, until I practically dropped, because I couldn't bear to see little children suffer in poverty like we had – going without food or water, being sick and dying alone on the streets or in makeshift huts. I was also driven by a promise I made to my mother, and so I had two little ones to care for and bring up. I had decided that they wouldn't face the poverty and the hardship that my sister Vanessa and I had faced as children.

The bank sent me on three global trips to publicise the work I was doing for charity in India. I was one of few girls – or maybe the only girl – from our community in India who was being flown around the world. When coming back, I was subjected to the envy of many, but many others looked upon me and said, "She's very blessed and she deserves everything she's worked so hard for." I always remembered my father's words once again – "Let not a person's opinion of you change the opinion you have of yourself!"

However, it was hard not to do this sometimes. I found, to my disappointment, that even amongst some of the professionals working for a global bank the small-mindedness existed and it was deep-rooted; very similar to the people in the slums of Kidderpore.

For some people working at the bank, the fact that I was recognised as a key part of the team by management – and also brought the country international recognition through going to some of the most deprived areas and working for the poorest of the poor, putting a smile on their faces – was not enough. Being an Indian-English girl who was doing well in her career led to the start of a whispering campaign amongst some of the more ignorant folk, insinuating that, being an Indian-English girl, I must be sleeping my way to the top.

Determination and very hard work is what gained me respect, what got me noticed and rewarded. It was most certainly not because of my being an Indian-English girl or a 'slut'. No amount of trauma, poverty, hard work or dedication could change the mindset of people. Even though many senior people respected me for what I truly was, the opinion of the ignorant minority never changed. I have come to realise that, irrespective of whatever social, economic or cultural background of a group of people, there is always the small minority who feel it necessary to pick on, highlight and often bully and abuse others, on the basis of any apparent difference to everyone else.

I know I have experienced this many times in my life, and I'm sure this is something anyone who is fairer, darker, fatter, thinner or different from others in any way will have experienced too. It took me many years and a level of maturity to understand that, in most cases, this is merely a reflection of their own insecurities and conditioning, caused by their past experiences, rather than any provocation or fault of the target of their ridicule or abuse.

At that time I was friendly with a boy I will call Shaun, who had been my friend for seven years. He was a genuinely nice person but not very career-focussed. There were two issues with that relationship. I was actually doing exceptionally well at the bank, and he felt inadequate in comparison.

People started to talk about him, saying snide things like, "She's doing very well and you're not." He used to get those comments from everyone around our social circle. No matter where he went, people would point this out to him. They didn't understand that he had bigger and better qualities, but given that this didn't fit into the accepted social model he ended up being on the receiving end of many jokes, for no real fault of his.

However, I think the major factor that broke us up was the fact that we never really did have a normal relationship, not one that was a natural flowing thing just between the two of us. We went from problems with my mother being very ill, to me taking over the two little ones. I focussed on my job, my charity work, my father and the lives of my younger siblings. Sad as it is to say, it seemed like I just lost track that he even existed – and, to be honest, I completely forgot about him. Shaun was a very good and kind person, and he was always quite happy to just be there for me.

Even though we cared for each other emotionally, we slowly drifted apart. When I told him I was leaving, he sat below my house for more than two weeks and wouldn't go home. He just wouldn't go, affirming, "You know I can't leave you. You can't leave me!" "This is life and we just have to break up. There isn't anything left," was my answer.

Today, I believe that people come into your life and leave it for a reason. Our needs were met, we learnt everything we needed to from each other, we took care of each other's parents, we grew spiritually and mentally as people, and it was time to move on. I once cared deeply for him, but, having moved on, I had bigger priorities and bigger things to do in life – and therefore the relationship was in no way sustainable.

One of the annual events I organised for all employees of the bank was a weekend away to a local tourist destination, as a sort of "thank you" to staff for all their hard work and effort the previous year. In 1999, shortly after I had broken up with Shaun, I arranged a trip for all staff to Agra, a short way away from our branch location of Delhi. Agra is, of course, famous for the Taj Mahal. We were lucky to reserve a hotel where the Taj was visible from the balconies and viewing galleries and, believe it or not, it was on one of those viewing galleries I first spent quality time with my future husband. We just seemed to get talking one evening, and before we knew it, we realised we were the only ones left there. The sun was about to rise; the whole night had passed without our noticing, both of us so absorbed in conversation!

When I met my future husband, I was happy that someone finally cared enough to look after me, that somebody wanted and was able to take care of me. I had seen him around in the bank before, but we had never really talked or interacted before that trip in Agra. He was a diligent bank professional. He was working fourteen to fifteen-hour days himself, as was I, and seemed focussed on his career. He seemed intelligent and well-read. We clearly took to each other, having a fair amount in common.

When we started to see each other, we were both very careful to be discreet about our relationship and not let it come in the way of our professional lives at the bank. However, word got around that we were seeing each other. Many people were happy for us both, but our relationship won him no respect from some quarters, especially when his boss Mr Katpalia found out that I was an Indian-English girl, and not Indian. If my husband ever asked to leave work on time or for a rare day off, I remember his manager constantly provoked him, saying that all he wanted to do was to see the 'Slut' – meaning me – and that he did not have the ambition to work hard.

This wasn't true as he was, and still remains, a very career-focussed person. He was on the phone to several clients even when he was out or driving with me. Over time, he had learned to look through his boorish boss's ranting. It didn't hurt any longer, and he dismissed it as the ignorance of an intelligent professional who, sadly, had no

176

social sense or manners. It did make me angry, because his boss didn't even know me.

Quite ignorantly, he and other people like him branded me, despite the fact that they didn't know how hard I had struggled since I was born; what sadness or grief I had buried inside me, the fact that I had two little ones at home who were not my kids but my siblings, and the fact that I worked incredibly hard for a reason. Before considering any of that in the slightest, people like him just shot their mouths off in order to get their own way or make their positions felt. Because he was the, then, head of some department in the bank, he took it that 'obviously' he held the right to speak and judge the way he did, even without knowledge, experience or fact. He never paused for a minute to think that he had no idea of what he was talking about, but he knew one thing extremely well – how to abuse and judge people.

He wasn't aware at all that the person he was dismissing as a 'slut' was just a simple girl born in India to British parents, a girl who had endured a world of hurt and humiliation due to no fault of her own. Yet she did not deserve to be called a slut by a man who knew not the object of his racism. He had never been taught better in the first place.

My husband and I got engaged to be married in the year 2000. His parents were professionals of note – university professors. Athough they spent part of their lives abroad, they were very much Indian at heart. I was not looked upon favourably, and neither was I readily accepted.

As is tradition in India they undertook to have my birth chart done, which said, by virtue of my date of birth, I spelt death for their son. My mother-in-law told me that I was a Manglik, which apparently means a girl who one day would be the death of her husband as we were star-crossed, or something like that. While my husband laughed and told me not to bother about this traditional mumbo-jumbo and that he did not believe it for a second, it did hurt me that educated professionals like my in-laws did not realise that saying this to someone just before they were married was quite hurtful.

I was made to feel like they were doing me a favour or taking a risk by allowing their son to marry me. Little did I know then that the idea was to make it known that nothing and nobody was above their son; and that, to start with, you've come in with a curse to the family.

I also started to notice differences in the way his family as an Indian family interacted with each other compared to the culture I was used to. For example, I noticed that even though my husband's mother was an intellectual in her own right and a respected university professor, she nevertheless appeared to be scared or timid most of the time, when her husband was around. While visiting us, she would not serve herself or allow me to serve myself unless the men were served first. It was very different from our culture, since ladies were always put first from where I came from. I struggled for a long time to try and understand this behaviour and to try and accept it, but I was always very sad for her. I made my sentiments clear to my husband, and further would not accept any of this behaviour myself.

I recall several times, when I was talking to her about my husband's illness, that my father-in-law walked in and just looked at her – and she either changed the topic, or just left the room. It was as though I was being told: this is how things are done, and you need to learn. I found it extremely difficult to cope under those circumstances, and was continuously upset to see another human being treated this way. To my husband, it was absolutely acceptable, and he found nothing wrong in it. To me it was as though I was being witness to another person's sadness, and not trying to do anything about it.

My husband was a juvenile diabetic. At the time we

met, he had already had the disease for approximately twenty years. Aspiring to be a normal youngster, yearning to feel part of teenage groups and fit in with a crowd, he didn't keep to his prescribed diets or healthy eating; therefore his condition had, over time, gotten worse. Shortly after we got engaged, he discovered that he had started to suffer the onset of complications of long-term diabetes – it was affecting both his optical and renal function.

I asked for some time before consenting to marry him. I needed to have some time alone and space to think of what I really wanted out of life. Things were happening too fast, and I hadn't had any time to think of what I wanted for myself. At this juncture, my father having moved to Delhi to stay with me was a large factor in my decision process. He was not yet even settled in before he reminded me of how he always wanted us to move to the UK, where he felt we would be more accepted and appreciated. I'm sure, deep down, he hurt for all the things we had been through, and just wanted us to be happier.

From the bottom of my heart, I very much wanted to move all of us to the UK. It had always been both of my parents' most fervent dreams. I had travelled in my charitable roles for the bank, and had seen developed parts of the world that were far more socially tolerant.

Although born in Calcutta, we were British by ancestry and by upbringing. When I started to travel around the world and see its variety of cultures, and mixed with other people, my perspective on life changed. I wondered what it would be like if I got my family away, and I made it absolutely my primary focus to locate our ancestry papers, to help my parents fulfil their lifelong dreams.

The main difficulty was that the papers were housed at a government ministry in London. The key to success would be to find all of our grandparents' papers, proving that we were English on both sides. At that time, I happily discovered that the couple who had looked after me had left for the UK. With ancestry similar to mine, their parents also being British, they had actually moved there.

They gave me the details for the Home Office and for the British Library, because any British people born in India at the time of the Raj had their birth certificates stored in the British Library in London. For all those who were born in Britain, their birth certificates were stored in the Home Office. Supplying me with the numbers and the addresses, they explained, "Look, we don't have much money. We've just got here ourselves, so we can't really help you in all this, but you might want to give it a go yourself." I most certainly wanted to give it a go. I was determined from that moment to get my family to the UK, to try to change our lives.

I was doing very well at the Bank of America. Luckily, for once, money wasn't an issue. I called up and I asked them to conduct a search for our ancestry papers. They said that they would search five years up and five years down from the date provided. If they didn't find anything I would lose my money, and would be required to pay again for the next search to be carried out. I paid for the first search but they never found anything. Then I paid for a second search, because I had to prove ancestry up to my grandparents. Somehow, I had to make the link that we were all British in order to be allowed entry into the UK, otherwise, we would not be granted British citizenship.

I just had to get those papers. I sat with my father, whose memory at almost eighty years of age was fading. I kept urging him on. "Dad, try and remember when Mum was alive. Where did her dad die? And how did he die? What was his full name and how old was Mum at the time?" I must have sat for weeks on end with him, simply trying to get any little detail that he could possibly remember.

I was very lucky because the woman who was talking

to me from the Home Office was very helpful. Getting my parents' birth certificates from the British Library was easy. They were obviously British, and because I knew their dates of birth, their certificates were there. Getting their parents' certificates, however, started to look almost impossible, lacking the exact dates of birth as I did. Without being able to link our ancestry with birth and marriage certificates, applying for immigration wasn't an option.

I was overjoyed and delighted the day she told me she had found it. She told me that she had found the marriage certificate as well, and now I had the complete chain. She mailed all the certificates to me by courier. She became so friendly and close to me that I sent her a bouquet of flowers once the certificates were found, to thank her for everything.

It was the month of May and everything was happening at once. I was overjoyed with the arrival of my family's ancestry papers. The family was electrified with excitement. Most of us wanted to go. Quite certainly I wanted to get myself, the children, and most especially Dad over to England.

Adding to the layers of plans and arrangements, I had made a decision about my betrothal, as you will find in the next chapter. I spoke to my boss, the CEO of Bank of America, and he was extremely open and gracious about it, genuinely happy for me. He said, "Don't worry. You've been with us for so long, and you've been so good to us, that I'm going to give you a redundancy package as a special favour to you. If anyone deserves to succeed, you do, and I will be there to help you every step of the way. It will help you with all your expenses when you go and settle there. I just want the best for you, so that's my favour to you."

Without question, he was very good to me. What he gave me was more than one and a half million rupees. It sent shockwaves throughout my system as I recalled the times under the stairs and when we could not afford the rent in Kidderpore for a mere 100 rupees, or a meal for five rupees.

Upon receipt of the courier package, the first thing I did was to go to my elder sister's house. I give her the papers asking her to apply for her visa, and to take her husband and her son with her. The return of the Haslams to England had begun. It was like winning the lottery!

Jill at different charities in India

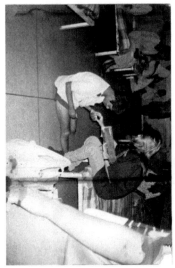

Jill at different charities in India

CHAPTER FOURTEEN:
PATHS OF TENFOLD ENDURANCE

One day, my husband took my father out for dinner. My father, having met him, and being a man of few words, had two things to say afterwards. I remember him looking at me with grave concern.

"Oh, he's a proper gentleman and I like him, but...!" he began, in the most caring manner ever. "Look, he's a really nice guy, but, there are two issues. The first is...you know...he's ill. I had a friend who was diabetic, and life just gets worse and worse if not kept under control. You've already had a very hard life. You've already done too much in a very short period of time, and I just hope that you don't have to take on any more; it might be the straw that breaks the camel's back. The boy has no idea of what you've been through, and has no idea of what he's about to put you through."

My father continued, "If my wisdom serves me correctly, you shouldn't underestimate the seriousness of his condition. By marrying him, you could be in for a life of something you're not ready to deal with. You have tenfold coming to you. So my advice to you would be not to marry him, because I know just how bad it can get, and I'm concerned for you."

He went on. "Another thing is that – as nice as he is – someone once said the East is East and the West is West, and the twain shall never meet. He's very different in far too many ways. You deserve to be with someone as loving and caring as you, and God knows you deserve to be happy, not live a life where your worlds do not connect – not to mention the abundance of sorrow and sadness that could come from coping with another illness of this magnitude."

At that time in life, one is very young, naïve and seldom listens or obeys their elders. I was swept off my feet with all the gifts and the attention, and with just experiencing great days after what seemed to be a lifetime.

"You know, I'm going to leave you with those words," my father concluded. "And you can figure it out for yourself. You're a big girl, now. But their world and our world are two different worlds – and no matter how cultured people are, or no matter how educated people are, there will always be differences. You are very different from him, in very many ways. It takes a lot more to make a marriage work than a few gifts and dinners."

Today, I realise the power behind those words. I read

somewhere that the best school in the world is at the feet of an elderly person, if only we choose to learn!

I remember thinking constantly about the importance of going away to London, and I told my husband, "Listen...I need some time to think of what I want to do. I need some time to get over a lot of things. It's going to mean a new job for me in the UK, and the UK itself is going to be new to me, too. I just need some time to come to a decision."

Despite my suggesting to him that he follow me to the UK later, he told me "You know I love you, and would like to come with you to make sure you settle in comfortably in the new place. We can start life there together."

I believe he actually did love me and really meant what he said, but neither he nor I could foresee the troubles that lay ahead. At that time, because I wasn't really witnessing the worst of it, I just hoped – and hope being a very big thing – that things would get better. I said, "All right, fine. Let's get married," and that was that. I was in the middle of coming to the UK and resigning from the bank, moving home, and also worrying about how all his medical tests went at the hospital. Without giving it much thought, we got married.

I understand today that one should never ignore the

words of parents, and I have paid a very heavy price in doing so. As I said, I was very vulnerable. I had huge responsibilities, and was tired and obviously very emotional, given my past experiences and the human suffering I had not only endured, but witnessed first-hand.

And I didn't listen. Undeniably, I do remember my father's words; though I can't do anything about it now. So I married him, and we moved to the UK, full of hope for new beginnings to start our lives together.

Unfortunately, as soon as he moved and registered with the local doctors in the UK, they changed his medication to the UK variety and did not really take the trouble to recalibrate his dosage. They probably didn't realise that he wasn't a stable case, and hadn't been on strict control for quite a while. They just transferred him over. As a result his condition got really bad, and for quite some time was very hard to control.

We later discovered that they had changed to a human form of insulin from bovine, and tolerance levels of the body for these types of insulin are dramatically different. As a result, he was turned into a person who would be absolutely normal one minute and in the throes of a severe attack of hypoglycaemia the next. Neither he nor I was aware of what was happening, and it was scary and frightening.

His condition was not good at all. It got so bad that, while he was at an interview for a senior role at a bank, his new medication caused him to pass out during the meeting! He was taken to hospital, where tests were carried out; he was in an unstable condition.

When we got married, I did not think I was marrying someone so unstable and ill. I could not see the person I thought I loved and married, but instead saw this person who was not in control of his own body and mind. We could not have anticipated how quickly things would spiral out of control, and we did not see what the future would be.

All I did see was that, clearly, lying before me there was a person who was suffering terribly, and who needed my help. Without even considering what it might lead to, I took it on with all my heart and soul. I wanted to ensure that his life was as comfortable as possible. I did everything I possibly could, and if there were some things I couldn't do then I tried to keep him happy enough at least to give him the confidence and the hope to go on. I had no idea of the consequences it would have on me or on the marriage.

My husband, being Indian, was very culturally different

from me. My own background was a maternal one, while his Indian background always had a strong paternal influence. Apart from coping with his illness and holding down very stressful jobs, we also had our different views and outlooks on various matters to deal with on virtually a daily basis, which made life even more challenging. This was something my father had warned me about.

Taking care of him, accepting his behaviour and his need to be in control, was just not enough. Paying the price by way of giving up many pleasures in my own life in order to support his just wasn't enough, either. With the amount of antibiotics, medication and all the dozens of side effects involved, it became impossible to deal with the person himself.

Sometimes, I felt that I couldn't cope. My sense of extreme depression, exhaustion, and the feeling of being let down yet again, were getting the better of me. I had to be so very patient with him, so forgiving and so forbearing, and I couldn't understand why it was me who had been put into this situation, yet again. There were times during his illness when he was unintentionally rude and nasty. Yet I had to always put it down to him being ill. I always tried to keep in mind that people are not their behaviours.

People commented that part of the problem might have been due to his ailment and the associated anger and trauma of not being able to lead a normal life, coupled with the amount of antibiotics that he had been prescribed. Clearly my attitude to him had changed as well – I went back into a shell of some kind. In his words, I went from 'the perfect loving girlfriend' to a 'cold, distant, yet sympathetic wife,' and this change hurt and frustrated him as well. Besides his illness and his sense of loss, some of his demanding and controlling behaviour, however, still came down to a matter of his upbringing, his culture, and his need to be in control of every situation.

His illness got worse as we went through every conceivable stage of hardship, pain and suffering, both mentally and physically. With every day we only hoped that it would be better than the last one, that his levels would remain stable. Even on nights when I could have slept I mostly lay awake, scared that his levels would drop so low that he would slip into a coma and might even die, just because I fell asleep.

It always reminded me of the time when, boiling in the heat and literally falling with exhaustion, I sat by my infant sister on the floor in the candlelight, fanning her and watching the clock in order to give her medicine every few minutes. I constantly worried that should the alarm of that old clock fail to go off just once, or I failed to wake up, she would die because of me. That was very traumatic back when I was only a little girl; our marriage situation now grew equally difficult, with me once again being placed in a position of life or death.

After those long and troubled nights, we would both wake up the next morning and go to high-pressured jobs in the city which made both of us very tired and stressed out. When we got back in the evenings he, at least, had a chance to rest, and often couldn't go on due to his illness – but I had to take on all the work at home and see that he was comfortable. This meant that for months at a time there was no rest for me, which made life impossible.

Since he was diabetic and we lived on a roller-coaster of high and low sugar levels, we hardly had a day of not having to either get the levels up or down. Sometimes I would need to rush to a station to help him get home safely, to the car to get him out, to get him off a train, or off a road. At times throughout his illness he became unpredictable, due to his levels playing havoc with him. He fought for survival, struggling for just a day to be normal, for people not to view him as being so ill; but none of that was easy or possible.

He may have been the one desperately ill, the one going through the physical turmoil and the agony of not being in full control of himself every time his levels went out of control, but I was the one who had to endure at every end. I merely existed...I wasn't living. Trying to cope the best I could, I sometimes found myself at breaking point. I felt cheated at times that I hadn't been warned by his family that it was going to be like this. Then again, no one could have known or even imagined that things would get so bad.

At the same time, he tried his best to keep his job, working as hard as he could despite everything that he was dealing with every day. He always held down a responsible job with leading organisations. He ensured that, despite his illness, he kept working so that we could maintain a good comfortable standard of living. If it meant he had to travel internationally while carrying dialysis bags to treat himself on the road, he did it with a smile, in order to ensure he fulfilled his duty as the man in the relationship.

He would often thank me for all I was doing for him. He would take hours to relax and calm down after a 'hypo' or a 'hyper' episode, and would suddenly go into a frenzy of destructive, unpredictable behaviour.

With the levels raging through him, almost in an instant he would sometimes change into this, hurtful and unkind person that I didn't even want to know. Unfortunately, I was so upset by all I was managing and going through that his best efforts were only like a drop of good in the ocean of despair I found myself drowning in. It felt like being with a man who had no control over his own emotions, a man who was mentally unstable, and yet capable of being caring when he was feeling well. It was impossible to feel loved and abused at the same time. I had to block out the bad in order to see the good and, more importantly, to be able to take care of him with much love and dedication.

When he did not get his own way, he resorted to sniping at me that I couldn't wait for him to die. These words were even harder to accept, and it was a good thing that I had experience in dealing with ill people in the past. I knew that they could and would say just about anything, but didn't really mean it. It stems from a feeling of despair, depression, insecurity and emotional turmoil.

Besides being exhausted after work and doing almost everything on my own, the burden was enormous to carry. I watched him night and day. I had to learn very quickly how to deal with such a sick person, how to revive him, and how to care for him long-term. We had not even married a few months when things got to an unbearable level. Here was another huge task to deal with.

On one hand, it wasn't very hard for me, because I had done it before. On the other hand, it was hardship of a different kind, and it felt even worse because I had had my fair share of it. I desperately longed for a few days of happiness, a few days of rest, which I never seemed able to find. It was desperation; frustration, anger, sadness, you name it. Emotions ran high without knowing whether to leave or stay, whether to give in or give up.

If anyone has ever lived with an ill person, they know just how hard existence could get. When you have to do it as many times in one lifetime as I have, with each occurrence lasting three to five years, it does take a toll on you in every possible aspect of life. There were months on end when I was lucky to have got a few hours sleep at night without having to wake up to see to his care, administer to his severe cramping, to his vomiting almost everywhere. I would change his bed linen, change his clothes, rush to get his medicine or to find a Coke really quickly, rub his ankles – doing whatever it took to make him feel comfortable.

Sometimes, I literally felt that I had a life in my hands and was dicing with death each and every day, while at the same time my life was slipping by faster than I knew. Apart from his suffering, which I always understood, I never failed to put myself in his place, to see it from his position. I thought about how difficult life was for me, but how much more difficult it was for him to be living with this illness.

Never for a moment did I ever forget this, and his parents ensured that it was kept that way. It was always about him and always about his illness. To them, I didn't exist. I could never feel unwell or exhausted, and I could never feel sad or alone. I always had to put him first. There was nothing that I could have gone through or felt that would ever be put down to being worse than what he was going through. In a nutshell, it was as though he was made of flesh and blood, and I was made of steel.

I noticed very early in the marriage that, despite his illness, he also had an underlying controlling streak. Many friends of mine in India have told me about their partners being the same way, but this is something I had never encountered myself. While he knew he was ill and needed care, he learnt very quickly that he could use that to get his own way.

I first witnessed this behaviour at his parents' house, where disrespect and emotional blackmail was the name of the game. My husband could say anything, do and behave in any way he wanted, and could get away with it. Firstly, because he was the youngest in the family, and secondly, because he was ill. His mother usually paid the biggest price, having to endure from both sides – from the father, and from the son. I initially thought that this was their individual family affair and that I didn't have the right to intervene, even though I walked out on many occasions, holding out until my husband apologised to her for his behaviour. I hurt for her, having to tolerate this from both sides.

What I did notice, however, was that every time he was rude and insulting, his parents always gave in a little more and always asked me to let it go, too. He could be extremely hurtful at times, and still I had to face him while he sat there, behaving as though he had done nothing wrong. I understood that they did this because he was their son and ill, and, therefore, he would usually get away with anything.

I also understood that they gave in even more to this adverse behaviour because of him being ill. They didn't want his levels to rise (be it diabetic or blood pressure or anything else), and so he got away with murder in the name of his 'illness'. I grew angry and resented this, as it was wrong and needed to stop. This was expected of me, as well. Every time his behaviour was uncalled-for and I refused to accept it, his illness got worse.

The physical aspect was extremely hard, but dealing with the mental aspect of things was where I found it impossible to cope. There was one incident when I was dressed for work and he prevented me from rushing out by grabbing onto my collar and pulling me back in, causing the buttons on my shirt to break. His sugar levels were very low at the time. The reason was just because he wanted me to have breakfast before rushing out, since I hadn't eaten that morning and he couldn't see that getting to work on time was more important for me than eating breakfast. Again, I put that down to his illness, and continued to remain with him in order to take care of him only because I knew that his behaviour often got irrational when his blood sugar levels were not normal.

I couldn't accept the way things were, and he couldn't accept it any other way. Things happened too fast and the blow was too severe for one to be able to cope with life, let alone concentrate on a happy married life. There were times when his behaviours even prevented my sister and me from being seen together, or taking the train and coming home together. We could not be seen talking to each other, due to the fact he felt alone and insecure. Rather than dealing with his behaviour, we chose to hide and meet each other. It was a terrible way to live, but we did it in order to keep him happy and to prevent upsetting him.

My husband couldn't see or appreciate, at the time, that his illness had caused him to appear to be a very different person than the person I loved. I therefore, at that point, had no feelings – perhaps apart from sympathy – for him in this changed condition.

My sister and I were living our lives with a man whom we often felt we didn't even know, and who probably didn't even know himself. We just coped, gave in, and managed to the best of our ability. There wasn't a day when tears didn't fall or fear didn't prevail. I was constantly scared of him being rude to her and my sister constantly hurt for the way I had to cope with things. Overriding our own happiness, however, we wanted nothing more than for him to get well and be happy. Somewhere, somehow, we survived each and every day of years of extreme human hardship, and managed in our own way to get through to him. We did have the choice of leaving him, but we were not brought up to abandon. We were taught to always consider another's position before we passed judgement on anyone. We were raised to love everyone, mainly those who were sick, suffering, and needed our help. It was very hard to be kept like prisoners in our own house, to be scared to talk, laugh or feel for each other, but we stood the test of time – and we won.

When my husband was on dialysis, it meant me dropping everything and rushing home from work. It meant me carrying up dialysis bags (thirteen and a half kilograms each) night after night, with an assortment of other medical equipment as well. He would want to help but I insisted that he was not in any fit physical condition to do so, and made sure I did this for him. Then I had to help him set it up on an eight-hour cycle of treatment, not to mention the dozens of other things that go with nursing an ill patient at home.

Some people say it is my fate and what was meant to be; that many couldn't deal with the amount of hardship and trauma that went with marrying such a person. Truly, he had no-one who could understand him and make him feel whole again. Therefore, you are sometimes chosen to carry out a role for a purpose. I believe that – whether or not it happened for a reason, or just because I allowed my heart to rule my head – no-one will ever know. To this day, I am not entirely sure; but I do believe that life is exactly what you make of it, and the choice was always mine. I made it and I had to live with it.

I only know that every year brought on even more mental and emotional hardship. And at every stage, our lives were turned upside down. It became impossible to go on and hard to believe that life was just not changing. It was, for me, being pushed from one door of intense human endurance into another. While I always believed that I would be very happy some day, I was also sometimes mortally afraid that I had no hope of ever being happy again. After leading such a hard life since the time I was a child and coming through it all, it was hard to imagine, let alone accept, that yet another tremendous task awaited me.

It is indeed a good thing that we are unable to tell the future. I would never have made it, but my parents always taught us that patience is what makes a man, and that people are too quick to give up on everything should it not work in the first instance. They don't wait to understand before ending something in order to secure their happiness, not realising that it's in unravelling the hardship that happiness is found.

Walking out, or even suicide, wasn't a way forward; even though I have to admit that I had contemplated it on more than one occasion. I now know that it is weakness.

Sadly, some of us become weak enough to succumb, and some of us move forward despite any adversity; and it is adversity that builds character.

Supporting him and making something out of my life at the same time were not incompatible, because I had done it before and could do it again. It might have been hard, but I didn't need to abandon someone or toss him aside in order to do it. I needed to find a way – to find the inspiration, the strength, and the ability to make it happen, despite anything that came my way. Part of me honestly believed that everything was happening for a reason, and that someday it would be this capacity for endurance which would change things forever. It's when you truly believe in something that miracles start to occur. As Mother Teresa put it: It's only when you believe that you become a pencil in the hands of God.

I started to study and, as they say, learning is not for information, but for transformation. I changed my thought processes from those of a suicidal wreck, to a person who believed that nothing could stop them. I wasn't going to let go that easily. I had to find a way, and I had to work even harder. I had to believe even more, and I had to find that inner strength in order to move on despite all odds. I had a good job but it was not what I truly wanted in my life, and

I was not going to settle for second best. The idea was to work with your core ability and experience and turn it into glory; not to wait for something you don't have while hating yourself and your life for not having it. I now know that everything we want is within reach, irrespective of our circumstances. It just all depends on how badly we truly want it.

I had dreams, aspirations, a goal, an objective, a passion, a purpose and a drive – but, with things the way they were, all of these aims couldn't have looked further away from being achieved at all. I knew one thing, though; I was not going to give up on my dreams. No one and no amount of hardship was going to make me give up. I knew that things were going to get even harder, but the mind is a powerful tool that can work for or against you. I learnt to forget the physical body, separate the emotions, and train the mind.

My husband was hospitalised in 2007 for a dual transplant (kidney and pancreas), and since then his condition has improved. Will my original feelings ever return? At this point it's far too early to say. I've been through too much and every time a memory rears its head it's very hard not to stop it from tapping into your emotions, but I have to admit that if things weren't so hard for so long, I wouldn't have been the person I am today.

Although he is trying to lead a life as close to normal as he possibly can, we still continue to deal with multiple issues that need care and attention. The idea was to learn how to put my circumstances second, and my life first. Not losing focus is the key to one's self-development.

My father used to say that maybe it was because I was born at home that he felt that I was different. A few weeks before he passed away, he said, "I do not know how to thank you for everything you've done for me and for the family, and for so many around you. But what I do know is that one day you will be blessed with more than you would ever need. You must remember never to give up on your dreams, and to continue to be who you really are."

He always reminded me of the poem by Edward A. Guest, You Mustn't Quit. My father loved to repeat the last few lines. Every time I was about to give up or was on the verge of a breakdown, I used to think of this poem and these words. They always gave me the ability to take that next step and to know that things would positively get better, but only if I held on. Stick to the fight when you're hardest hit. It's when things seem the worst that you mustn't quit.

As William Barclay once said: Endurance is not just the

ability to bear a hard thing, but to turn it into glory.

I intend to do just that.

CHAPTER FIFTEEN:
IN LONDON TOWN

Soon after moving to the UK I helped the rest of my family to move here, too, except for a brother and a sister who remained in India. Before marriage, I had informed my husband-to-be that my one most fervent desire was to help my family to move to the UK, and, what's more, my two younger siblings would stay with me until such time as they got on their feet.

This soon became a point of friction between us, as a new couple. We had barely settled into the country when, only three months later, my younger sister moved in with us permanently. She was then followed by my two other sisters, one after the other, who stayed with us for about six months each and then moved out on their own.

I do believe that things happen for a reason, in great measure. However, the fact that my youngest sister came to live with us was a godsend, because she helped me through a lot. On most occasions I would not have managed to go on, if I hadn't had another person's help at hand.

It got to a stage where I could not go and spend quality

time with my family very often, and would always feel compelled to make excuses for them not to come over. Firstly, he didn't want them to see him unwell; therefore, the less they knew or saw, the happier that made him. Secondly, I didn't want him to be rude and unkind to them, so just made excuses and kept them away. It was easy on him, but very hard on me.

Over time I grew more distant from his family – except from his brother, who is an exceptional human being and has always reached out to me. I felt that I wasn't getting the help and understanding from them that I expected. They did not like a girl spelling things out or talking about any personal issues. This was unacceptable behaviour. If you didn't adhere to policy, you were branded as not being normal. Normal to them was to endure, and to endure in private. They called it adjustment. To me, being sick was no shame, and therefore it wasn't a problem to speak about it; but I wasn't allowed to do so, not even to my own family.

To discuss his illness with his own parents was taboo. The task was pretty simple where they were concerned. You didn't ever talk about their son's illness, or what really went on behind closed doors, in public. You didn't express your feelings. You didn't speak of or share anything with strangers. They believed that, now we were married, I should endure and continue to endure in silence. If I covered the whole thing up to make it look rosy, then I would have been behaving like one of the family. If I did the opposite, I would have been shut out in the cold as though I didn't exist – and that's exactly what was done. All I wanted to do was to talk to someone, and I desperately needed help.

As a result of our communication being more intermittent it became impossible to even speak to them about their own son, let alone get any help, advice or guidance. They refused to discuss the problem under any circumstance. Whenever I did get an opportunity to speak to them it was always about feeding him, how to take care of him, how to be nice to him, how to watch him, how to get him to the next doctor, how to let things go, how to be more tolerant, how to be more patient and – not forgetting – how I must adjust.

Not ever do I recall them asking how I was or how I was coping. They knew full well that I was at breaking point on many an occasion, but they never once asked if they could help or how I felt. Whenever I myself was ill or needed help, they always took the stance of "We don't interfere in the marriage." They simply didn't want to hear anything about how sick I was or how unhappy I was. I guess a woman wasn't expected to get sick or sad or tired, according to them.

Were they to ask, it meant they admitted that I had become that way because of the task at hand, and therefore they always avoided any conversation when it came to me. It felt like all they were interested in was their son. That was natural, but I was a life, too. They stubbornly refused to believe or acknowledge anything that might be adverse in relation to their son. It was as if they were telling me silently that it was custom to endure, and that I didn't have a choice. That's how it was, and I was not toeing the line. If I wished to speak to them, I must speak about only what they wanted to hear – not what I wanted to tell them. The amount I did for him, or the fact that I gave up my life to save his, was of little or no consequence to him or to his parents.

Although, I must admit that, in the heat of the moment, one who is emotionally wrought does not stop before they abuse someone to think of what those words could do to another person. Just like any other couple, we have had our words, our allegations and our beliefs – topped, of course, with a huge amount of health and behavioural problems to deal with. But some people know when and where to hurt in order to try and control you; to make you believe that, despite everything, you have the issues, because you came from nothing, financially, and are hence capable of nothing better. It is especially painful to that person if she has helped save your life on a number of occasions and has stuck with you no matter what. I am aware that millions live like this, but I had come too far to allow someone else's words or opinions to make or break me. Instead, there is greatness in forgiveness. If only you can get yourself to the point of forgiving anyone, irrespective of their words or actions, and instead look for something good, then there is always something to be found.

When you did what he wanted and were nice to him, in those cases he was nice too, saying things like, "If there was ever a pageant for the beauty of the soul, you would win hands-down." Could I believe these words? I didn't really know, but that proves the point that there is indeed something good in everything we see. I had a life to save and a duty to perform, and I did it with much love and care. On the other hand, despite his anger, resentment and the hurt he caused us, he was grateful. That took a lot of time to surface; but it eventually did.

While I do have to admit that he is very bright and

knowledgeable in many respects and also a very strong individual to have made it through this far, I put it down to a belief being a belief. Like a million other people, he could not change what had been instilled in him since he was a child, and those aspects came through on many occasions.

As I mentioned above, one cannot blame an entire race for what happens. In my case, while my family and I have been through a great deal in India, it does not mean that one should not be thankful and grateful for everything else. Yes, we did witness some awful situations and we were put through some very terrible – almost unendurable – times. But one of the biggest virtues in life is to be grateful for receiving the smallest tendering of a good deed. While the majority of them discriminated against us, there were a few who cared, irrespective of our colour, our country, or our race.

They looked upon us as human beings: as little children, as struggling parents, as people who were starving and in need of a shelter, as anyone who may ever need help of any kind. Whether it was a bit of meat that was given to us free, or a tiny loaf of bread, or a few overripe tomatoes that couldn't be sold; whether it was the school that took us in free of cost, the people who felt sorry for us and gave us a rupee or two to buy something to eat, the men who made us dance for a little treat. The man who give us ash to wash our dishes or the owner of a little tea shop who filled our bowl with diluted milk, or even the local chemist who gave us free medicines when we were in dire need — the deeds themselves were our salvation. If everyone thought the same and behaved in the same way as the people who abused us, we would never have survived those times. All of it, every tiny gesture of kindness, is what saved our lives.

I always cherish Elton John's song, 'The Circle of Life', especially the line that says Never take more than you give. Those words are invaluable. They remind me of all the extremely poor people who never had much of anything, but always shared what they had. To me it means even more because I know the value of a bit of bread, a biscuit, a sweet, a torn blanket, a toy, an old pencil, a decent pair of knickers – or even just having a place to sleep.

Those smallest tokens of humane generosity enabled me to have lived to tell this story.

For that reason alone I always make it a point to go back to look at the place I once lived in. It's there that we learnt some important lessons. It's that place that made us strong and taught us the value of life itself. The place that is not even fit for pigs to live in. A place that is worse than any amount of squalor and poverty that you could ever imagine. Places that people here wouldn't even pass through, let alone go to the toilet in, are places that I call home.

Despite everything, to me, those places are sacred. For me it's like going down a passage that holds some very dark heart-breaking memories – but some very happy ones, too – even though I am very grateful for what I have today, and have what many people could only wish for. The reality is that, no matter how sad the conditions, the abuse and the suffering were, it turned me into a person who values life to its fullest, and taught me never to look down at another person. I believe that life is the biggest blessing, and to be able to acknowledge who you truly are and where you came from, without feeling ashamed of your past, is what separates the mediocre from the exceptional.

I watched my mother go hungry for days, pretending that she was full. Then my sister and I started to do the same, so that the little ones could eat whatever little there was. We knew that it was nowhere near enough for even one child, let alone for four and our parents. We were trained to starve, to share every little we had, and to be grateful for whatever we had been given.

When you live not knowing if you'll make it through to the next day because of hunger and starvation, you then understand the value of survival and life itself. It's only then that you understand the bond that exists to save a loved one at any cost; even though you have nothing to offer except for love, and intense hope.

In the whole scheme of things, I may sometimes hurt when I think of all that others did to us, even though they had no idea of what we were constantly suffering already. They may not have thought of us as little children who held no malicious intent whatsoever. They may not have thought of us as even being human. Be that as it may, the help we got from the poorest of the poor was something that cannot be described, and cannot be forgotten. Through it all, their goodwill was a ray of hope that engendered in us the will to survive.

It is in loving response to that handful of people, who might have well forgotten us by now but whom I have never forgotten. I have been helping many others, both while I was in India and after I moved to the UK, but could never repay them for magnanimously saving our lives. The little we got during those days was immeasurable. If we never had received it, we could have died of starvation, of dreaded diseases, of malnutrition or so much more, in the same way that many of my siblings died. I believe that we have taken much more by way of our lives than what we've given back.

Therefore, here is my biggest wish. I wish to try to give back as much as I can to as many as I can in any part of the world (especially to the people in India), to all those who have suffered and are still suffering in very much the same way we did. My main objective and desire is to help people realise that their circumstances are not their reality, and that almost any hardship can be reversed and turned into unimaginable success.

CHAPTER SIXTEEN:
JOURNEYS OF A WITNESS

I have lived in the UK since the year 2000, and continued my career in banking. When I left India, I was running the Country Manager's office and was designated a Public Relations Officer for the bank. I was clearly valued and appreciated by the bank's management, which was demonstrated by the fact that I was compensated generously for my work at a level equivalent to some senior managers within the bank.

When I moved to London, however, I was surprised to find that my work experience and level counted for little in this market. In a way, I was compelled to re-establish myself in my professional field, while also undertaking the challenges in my personal life I have talked about earlier.

I can clearly recall a time when I was asked to do tasks like popping to the corner shop to get some milk for the office tea, or to deliver files to another office across the road, or even to refill senior managers' water bottles – which was hardly what I would have expected of my role as an Office Manager, or would have thought I would be doing once I had moved to the professional environment in the city.

I remember a few years later telling a colleague about it and she was shocked at some of this, saying that, if it had been her, she would have told them where to get off. However, I have always lived by the principal popularised by Maya Angelou: I can be changed by what happens to me, but I refuse to be reduced by it.

I found that over time this attitude of not feeling small or humiliated has always helped me grow in the long run. Slowly but surely, I've found that taking things in my stride and keeping my focus on delivering the best that I could to every situation got me recognised, until I found myself back to a position where I was the Office Manager for the global corporate office of a leading bank, and ran the administrative and support functions for them.

I always tried to learn from every situation I found myself in. I recall an instance where I was asked by the global head of a bank to buy tea and samosas, and to then get water for him too. I had all the right to refuse, but I always think of it as: if I wanted to have a snack I would go and get it, so what's the harm if I got some for my colleagues too? It might not be the snack of my choice but it doesn't matter. It's when you try to see the good in everything that you don't feel so bad and you prevent the negativity from harming you. Self-worth is worth much more than a few samosas.

I recall another occasion when a global CEO requested me to come to a boardroom with her coat and bag. When I went to deliver it to her, I was obliged to wait and stand within the room, holding her coat for over twenty minutes while she finished off her meeting. I tried to hang the coat up on the coat-stand but she asked me to keep holding it. She was sending a message to her team, who watched her behaviour with disgust, but I was more than happy to be of assistance to someone who was a CEO. Remembering the words of Warren Buffet: It takes 20 years to build a reputation and just five minutes to ruin it. I thought to myself that if she knew that, she would have acted differently.

While I stood there, I was watching with interest how she managed the different personalities and types of people in the room, while effectively getting her message across. At the end of the discussion, when she turned to me to apologise about keeping me waiting, I told her quite genuinely that it wasn't a problem and that I enjoyed observing her interactions with the team. She seemed to appreciate this. From that day on, we had a quiet, unspoken bond of trust between us, that exists to this day.

I suppose I could have felt belittled and humiliated by being made to stand there just holding on to her coat and bag, especially when I own a three storey house myself and have two maids that work for me, but I strongly believe that you should not let your current circumstances impact what you can learn from a situation. I have practiced this belief many times myself; and, more recently, as I have started coaching others as part of my business, this is something that many people have found very useful as well. There will always be difficult situations and difficult people, but there is also always a lesson to be learnt. Again, I quote the brilliant words of Warren Buffet: It's better to hang out with people better than you. Pick out associates whose behaviour is better than yours, and you'll drift in that direction. I considered myself lucky to be there, lucky to observe the different personalities, and lucky to learn from such senior individuals.

Over time, I found professional success and recognition. It was gratifying, and lent some stability to my life during those tough initial years after I moved to London – but in spite of all the success and recognition, I felt that there was something that was missing for me.

When I worked at Bank of America and used to go out into the slums, the children there would give anything just for a sweet or a biscuit. They reminded me of my siblings and myself. I often thought that if even half the amount of things here in the UK were given to less fortunate children there instead of being thrown away, the joy and the happiness that it would bring would be unimaginable.

How one sweet or one biscuit can feel when you're starving is impossible to understand for someone who has never had to starve, or to someone who can afford to buy dozens of different types of biscuits or sweets. I'm proud to have seen the results of both giving and receiving in this manner, and even more proud to acknowledge the fact. The most beautiful thing in the world to me is to see a child who can sit-up or stand or even smile once fed, after having starved for days on end.

From a very young age I found that I was at my best when I was helping others achieve their goals, or putting a smile on the face of someone less fortunate than me. It was this feeling of contentment and satisfaction that I missed during the initial years in the UK. I was continuing to help many people in India, using my own resources wherever possible. I have been supporting a few elderly ladies for over ten years now as well as helping many people in need who reach out to me in times of trouble and distress, but I know that the few I help from my own resources barely scratches the surface in terms of the number of people who still are in a bad way, and could use the help and the support.

I have witnessed innumerable scenes of people lying on the floor, literally covered in flies, with their little kids looking on. Millions of people bear diseases with no one to even touch them, leave alone feed them and comfort them. We ourselves suffered miserably throughout childhood; like the hordes of kids I've seen who, out of starvation, are too weak to even open their mouths to eat,, whose limbs are severed in exchange for a meal. Families are ripped apart, because there are just no means for surviving together.

I have held and cried with deaf and dumb teenagers who were being abused everyday by men of power and status. These poor souls have no one to defend them, much less to even give them a hug or something to smile about. I have held children between the ages of three and ten who have been starving for days, raped by their own relatives, and who don't have a hope in the world or even a meal, let alone a chance of being saved from a life of utter poverty and misery. I have sat for hours on end with aged people on the footpath, who are just in need of a shelter and some clothes, who have neither the will to go on or the strength to even talk. I have participated in and watched scenes that would shock the world if only they cared enough to want to know. Yet, even if they never want to see, nonetheless they are aware of the dire reality of human existence.

I fail to understand how people continue to live everyday without being aware of what is actually happening on our very own planet. While I understand that it isn't easy to relate to such situations unless you've actually lived it, I fail to understand how people say that they feel very fortunate to have the lives they have, and yet don't stop for a moment to think of just how unfortunate millions of people still are. It's truly amazing to think of how self-focussed we can be.

I have found, to my disappointment, that many people who set up charities nowadays sometimes deceive the poor. I have witnessed this first hand when I was heading the charity network at Bank of America. A few are genuine, but it is nowhere near enough to help even one tenth of the people who need it. Those that want to help cannot bring themselves to ask for donations, which is understandable given the stigma already attached to charities. Given my passion was to work in this manner, to help people who truly need it, it grieves me to say I've experienced this sordid state of affairs where it was impossible to ask people for any kind of help. Therefore I know that, since I am passionately driven to do it, I must do it on my own.

From a young age I was determined to make life better for those around me. I now wanted to do this with all my time and effort. I knew helping others change their lives gave me great satisfaction and that I had an inherent talent for this. I had always been the one my family, friends and colleagues turned to for help and advice, and they always found my support helpful in overcoming life's challenges.

But I knew I had to move this to a professional level in order to help many more people, and also do something for the many unfortunate people who are stuck in poverty and badly need help, in countries such as India. I had decided that I truly wanted to make this change.

To achieve my goal I studied further, and found that there were many techniques and methods to help people get the best out of their lives, and use their inherent skills to achieve what they truly wanted. I was pleased to discover that many of the things I had done naturally to help and comfort those around me actually had a scientific basis. Equally, some of the things we instinctively do are not the best way to help ourselves.

For example, I found that many people felt constrained by their upbringing, background and environment. I do recall a colleague who was concerned by her young kids being influenced by bad company at school saying to me helplessly "I don't really think I can help it. After all, they say Man is a product of his environment." I remember telling her that this wasn't necessarily the case and, if she ensured her kids had the right principles and values at home, the things they were learning outside would be less of an influence on them.

I was pleased to find that this actually has a basis in life-improvement whereby the human brain, in simple terms, has only the capability to bring forth more of what it is focussed on. One's future is not determined by one's past, but is influenced by one's desires and actions that are initiated by one's thoughts alone. This is articulated in the teachings of Abraham Hicks: What you think about, you bring about. It is also in the teachings of the Bible: As a man Thinketh, so is he!

It is not possible to always control what happens in life, but it is always possible to choose how you react to your immediate circumstances. I find that many people are unable to achieve their truest potential due to being affected by deeds that have happened in their past. They accept this fact, turn it into a secure belief, and seal their fate. This little issue is something that acts like a stopper on a champagne bottle.

My studies have taught me that it isn't about bringing yourself to forgive someone. In many cases we say we do forgive, but our words and actions prove otherwise. It's in understanding the difference between forgiveness and being able to let go for one's own self-development. That is actually key to removing the stopper, and becoming unstoppable.

My sister (a teacher) struggles with having to consciously tell every child that their performance has been exemplary, even when they have failed miserably. I have also noticed how most people only say what they think others want to hear, even if they don't honestly believe it or feel it. This behaviour I understand to a degree. It helps with insecurity issues; but successful coaching helps with bringing out the best in people, while pointing out how they can improve. As Johann Wolfgang von Goethe said: If I accept you as you are, I will make you worse; however, if I treat you as though you are what you are capable of becoming, I help you become that.

I noticed throughout my career how people around me

base their lives on 'titles', and will say and do almost anything in order to gain that title. Without it they feel empty, instead of recognising the greatness within themselves and the talents they possess. It's the title that makes them feel superior, and it's the same title that, when taken away, ends their entire world.

I learnt, early on, from a speech I once heard by Mark Sanborn. He said, "You do not need a title to be a leader. A lot of great leadership happens around the world by non-titled leaders. To name a few are Princess Diana, Oprah Winfrey – or Mahatma Gandhi, in fact. A person just needs the confidence to be the best that they can be, which is when no title matters any longer."

Over four and a half years I studied and qualified as a Life Improvement Trainer, a 'success coach', and a 'thought leader'. Apart from also acquiring other self-development credentials, I felt I now had the necessary qualifications, coupled with my own experience of overcoming adversities and difficulties, to help others succeed.

The one thing that became ultimately clear to me while I was studying is that, for all the training, coaching and other help that is available to anyone who is looking to succeed, ultimately one has to truly want to change their lives. All the help available can only support a person once they have made the key decision to help themselves. Recognising this key goal, I set up a Life Improvement and Training Company which I have called Help Yourself Associates, to help people improve their lives in order to reach their true potential.

As I launched this business and started to interact with my clients and tried to help them achieve their goals, I often used examples of how I had reacted in similar situations in order to help them relate to what they had to do to achieve a particular outcome. After all, if I could change my life from living under the stairs with no hope at all to becoming an entrepreneur, an author, a motivational speaker, running my own business whilst living the life of my dreams by being able to help others – there is no reason why anyone cannot do the same.

I have always been inspired by H.W. Longfellow's poem 'The Psalm of Life', that says:

> *Lives of great men all remind us*
> *We can make our lives sublime,*
> *And, departing, leave behind us*
> *Footprints on the sands of time;*
> *Footprints, that perhaps another,*

Sailing o'er life's solemn main,
A forlorn and shipwrecked brother,
Seeing, shall take heart again.
Let us then be up and doing,
With a heart for any fate;
Still achieving, still pursuing,
Learn to labour and to wait.

If, after reading this book, someone is inspired and pursues and achieves a better life for themselves and those around them, I believe these pages would have served their purpose.

AFTERWORD:
ABOUT THE AUTHOR

JILLIAN HASLAM IS THE AUTHOR OF INDIAN.ENGLISH, A MEMOIR about her early life spent as part of a forgotten minority of British people who were left on the streets of Calcutta after Indian independence, and the perseverance and triumph of spirit and will, that led her to success. After spending close to twenty years forging a successful career in the banking industry, Jillian decided to devote her energies to helping other people improve their lives. She is the founding Director of Help Yourself Associates, a life improvement and training company. Jillian is also a published author and popular motivational speaker who uses her own life experience to inspire others to never give up on their life goals, and shows them the way to achieve them.

Jillian overcame a childhood of abject poverty, racial abuse and hardship, taking on adult responsibilities while still a child, and dealing with sickness and death throughout her life – including the loss of four infant siblings and her mother when she was very young. In spite of these hurdles, she carved out a successful career for herself, raised her younger siblings, and never lost sight of her purpose in life. If anyone knows what it takes to rise above circumstances and seize control of one's life, Ms Haslam does. The essence of that indomitable spirit can be found throughout the pages of Indian.English.

Since moving from India to the U.K. in 2000, Jillian has turned her attention to learning how she can help others overcome challenges in life the way she has.

Jillian is a qualified Life Improvement Trainer, a Success Coach and a Thought Leader. She has spent many years learning about life skills and their application. She has used these principles to help change her own life. For the past several years, she has embarked upon the mission of using this knowledge and experience to help others change theirs. Her perceptive insight is matched by her many areas of accomplishment, which enables her to travel the world, meeting with people and inspiring them to change their lives by achieving the goals they have always sought.

Through Help Yourself Associates, Jillian currently offers her services in the areas of life improvement training, community out-reach programmes, life change certifications, public speaking and private counselling.

You can find out more about Jillian and her work by visiting www.helpyourselfassociates.com

Jill today

Lightning Source UK Ltd.
Milton Keynes UK
UKOW050626170212

187461UK00001B/10/P